Train Your Puppy

IN 8 WEEKS

T0273608

ACKNOWLEDGMENTS

I want to thank all of the dog owners and their dogs who, through their pictures, helped to make the first edition of this book a reality. To photographer Beverly Walter, I send my great appreciation for the wonderful shots she captured with her camera. She worked patiently for long hours just to record the best photo possible in every situation. Her talent and tenacity show. To my editor, Andrew De Prisco, I extend equal gratitude. He's a very patient leader and a wonderful organizer of his writers' words! I appreciate your knowledge and talent, Andrew. To all of them, my heartfelt "Thank you!"

—Charlotte Schwartz

TRAIN YOUR PUPPY IN 8 WEEKS

CompanionHouse Books™ is an imprint of Fox Chapel Publishing.

Project Team
Managing Editor: Gretchen Bacon
Editor: Joseph Borden
Technical Editor: Susan Ewing
Proofreader: Kelly Umenhofer
Designers: Mary Ann Kahn and Wendy Reynolds
Indexer: Jay Kreider

ISBN 978-1-62187-224-5

Library of Congress Control Number: 2022952155

This book has been published with the intent to provide accurate and authoritative information in regard to the subject matter within. While every precaution has been taken in the preparation of this book, the author and publisher expressly disclaim any responsibility for any errors, omissions, or adverse effects arising from the use or application of the information contained herein. The techniques and suggestions are used at the reader's discretion and are not to be considered a substitute for veterinary care. If you suspect a medical problem, consult your veterinarian.

Fox Chapel Publishing
903 Square Street
Mount Joy, PA 17552

We are always looking for talented authors. To submit an idea, please send a brief inquiry to acquisitions@foxchapelpublishing.com.

Printed and bound in China

Train Your Puppy

IN 8 WEEKS

A POSITIVE GUIDE FOR DOG OWNERS

CHARLOTTE SCHWARTZ

COMPANIONHOUSE
BOOKS

CONTENTS

Introduction to
Puppy Training

There's a new excitement in your life these days. It brings an automatic smile to your face every time you think of it. It's got a soft, furry coat, a wagging tail, and a wet nose. It's a puppy!

Regardless of the breed of dog you have—a tiny Chihuahua, a giant St. Bernard, or an all-purpose mixed-breed—the pup will need training. Naturally, the first kind of training we think of with a puppy is house-training, but that's only the beginning. You can house-train a puppy in a few short weeks at the most. Training him to live with you in harmony will take a lot longer.

Training for good manners and a lifetime of companionship will require knowledge, patience, and a desire to develop this puppy into a wonderful canine friend. If possible, you and your puppy should enroll in a puppy-training class in your neighborhood. Sometimes, however, attending a puppy class just isn't feasible. Perhaps there isn't such a class in your area or your work schedule prohibits your attending one. Another possible reason

THE CRITICAL PERIOD

Between birth and eight weeks of age, a puppy needs to be with and learn from his littermates. A puppy between 8 and 16 weeks of age is going through what is known as the critical period. This is the time when the puppy needs to be introduced to the outside world: to people, fellow canines and other pets, and to new experiences. Between 8 and 12 weeks, the puppy should be removed from his birth pack and brought into a human pack, where he will bond with the new owners. Ideally, the puppy should begin his education before he's 16 weeks old.

might be that you don't feel comfortable with the methods used in a local class or don't particularly care for the person teaching the class. Whatever the reason,

Everyone wants to have a well-trained companion dog that is a joy to own and fun to live with. Let's embark on our eight-week course towards an obedient and biddable pet.

you find that an organized class is not an option for you and your new puppy. Fortunately, there is another way to train your puppy—and you are holding it in your hands.

I've written this book for you. I've taken all the behaviors you may want to teach your puppy and presented them in an easy-to-follow sequence from week to week, just as if you were in a class with your puppy. The lessons from day one to their conclusion will help you to build a bond that will encompass all aspects of your lives, while you will get insight into the puppy's various developmental stages and his physical and intellectual potential. Training now, while the puppy is young, is the optimal time to develop desirable habits and a line of communication between the two of you that will last a lifetime.

Puppies are like sponges. They soak up knowledge and habits as quickly as they encounter each life experience. Furthermore, their bodies don't produce hormones until they are five or six months old. Without hormones, a puppy's attention is centered on you, his owner, rather than on other dogs and things that shouldn't concern him. For example, a young puppy will follow his owner wherever he goes and will be reluctant to wander off by himself. As the dog develops into maturity, his range of interest increases and curiosity incites him to wander away from his owner and often into potentially dangerous situations.

If we take a young puppy and teach him what we want him to know before his body begins to produce hormones, success will come easier than if we do this after the onset of hormonal development. A young puppy can be compared to a piece of clay in the hands of a potter. New clay can be molded into the finest object because it has no other elements to impair its beauty. However, once the clay is cluttered with debris, it's more difficult to mold it into a piece of fine art.

The proper way to hold a puppy is by using one hand to support the chest area and the other hand to support the rear quarters and hind legs.

MOTIVATING PUPPY

Motivators are anything your puppy wants. For most dogs, food is the primary motivator. There are, however, many other things that can serve to motivate your puppy: a favorite toy, an enjoyable activity such as a ride in the car or a walk on the beach, a gentle cuddle from a special person, a trip to the ice cream shop, or a play session with a favorite dog friend. These are all things you can use to encourage your puppy to focus on you and learn his lessons well. Actually, motivators become the rewards for learning, so we must be sure to make the motivators we use very desirable things.

Puppies are especially enjoyable and easy to work with when they are young because they haven't lived very long and thus haven't had the chance to develop a lot of bad habits. So teaching and nurturing desirable behaviors at the earliest opportunity will help to produce a superior canine companion.

This book will help you, the new puppy owner, to do just that. From the first to the final chapter, it explains how dogs learn and how to teach your puppy good manners. In addition, it offers a host of useful behaviors for control in and around the home, as well as in unfamiliar places. It suggests ways to help your puppy develop self-confidence so that he'll be able to cope with whatever situations he may face in his life with you. And it's all done with highly motivational methods to help your puppy enjoy his lessons.

To instill good manners in a dog, it is best to begin training when the puppy is young and more easily molded.

Three mighty "P"s are required to train your young dog: patience, praise, and practice.

This puppy is making eye contact with the photographer. This probably indicates that he will be a confident and attentive student.

You'll teach your puppy to sit, stand, lie down, stay, come when he's called, and walk nicely beside you without pulling on the lead. He'll learn to sit still for grooming and to wait patiently while you prepare his meal at feeding time. He'll learn to greet people without jumping up on them, to go to his own space, and to wait there whenever the need for control arises. He'll learn what is and is not acceptable behavior in the eyes of his owners.

How would you like your puppy to grow up and become a helper to you around the house, doing things like carrying in the mail, retrieving the newspaper from the yard, fetching your slippers, or bringing you his collar and lead when it's time to go out? Laying the foundation for these behaviors and many more are included in this book. I've even included a few tricks to teach your dog just for fun.

Add patience, praise, practice, and a pleasant attitude to the material herein and you'll have yourself a wonderful companion that will bring you pleasure for many years. So enjoy your puppy and enjoy learning together. Let's get started!

Puppy Training
Before You Begin

SUCCESS IN HOUSE-TRAINING

As with everything in life, success is a goal that everyone pursues, no matter the field, whether it's a career, a relationship, a business endeavor, or something as simple as training a puppy. Success that comes by luck is usually a happenstance and doesn't last. Success that results from carefully planned, proven methods is often more easily accomplished and lasting. It's this kind of success that you are seeking when it comes to house-training your pup. The author has developed the "Success Method" to provide the puppy owner with an easy-to-follow yet proven way to assist the new puppy in developing clean living habits and a feeling of security in his new environment.

The choice of where you want your puppy to relieve himself is entirely up to you, though it will be dependent upon your living environment. For example, city dwellers often train their puppies to relieve themselves along the curbside because large plots of grass are not readily

Potty training pads are an alternative to outdoor potty training, but can also be used as a stepping stone toward being fully house broken.

available. Or, they choose to train inside the home with helpful tools like potty training pads. These pads are absorbent and easy to change out throughout the day. Suburbanites, on the other hand, usually have yards to accommodate their dogs' needs.

In house-training dogs, I prefer to use a relief command, a catch-phrase

Perhaps Russian puppies are more difficult to train than American ones! As Pavlov seems to indicate, this Borzoi pup would need to practice a command 42 times before he could master it.

Take your puppy out frequently for toilet relief. Use a command such as "Potty time" or "Go make." Keep in mind that other people might overhear your command if you take the dog out for a walk, so don't choose a command that you'll feel silly repeating.

that will trigger to the puppy to know that it's time to "do his business." You will use this command each and every time the puppy needs to relieve himself (even if he's already in the throes of it). Some examples of relief commands are "Go hurry up," "Potty time," and "Go make." Choose a command that you are comfortable with, one that won't embarrass you if you have to use it in polite company or public.

You will get in the habit of talking to the puppy before you lead him to his relief area by asking him, "Is it potty time?" or "Do you want to go hurry up?" Once the puppy

has matured, you will know when he needs to "go" by simply asking him the question. While the puppy will understand your question, he cannot answer you back in words like "I sure do," but he will give you some tell-tale doggy signs, such as running to the door, barking, wagging his tail, etc.

Consistency is the key to house-training, and to all training, for that matter. You will always use the same relief area, you will always use the relief command and you will always take him there on his leash. All dogs welcome structure and consistency. By providing these, your dog understands exactly what is expected of him.

By following the Success Method as described here, your new charge will be completely house-trained by the time his muscle and brain development reach maturity. Keep in mind that small breeds usually mature faster than large breeds, and certain breeds are more difficult to house-train than others. Most breeders admit that male puppies, more fixated on their scatological functions, take more time than female pups. Regardless of these factors, all puppies should be house-trained by six months of age.

Understanding What Your Puppy Needs

Like human babies who do not have any control over their bodily functions, puppies haven't yet fully developed their intestinal tract muscles and must relieve

ON WHAT GROUNDS?

Possible outdoor surfaces on which to house-train your puppy will vary, though grass is the preference of most dog owners and dogs. Other surfaces include cement, blacktop, dirt and gravel. Depending on the breed of dog you have, gravel may not be ideal since some dogs tend to eat it. A disadvantage of blacktop is that it gets very hot in the summer months. Indoor surfaces most

often mean potty training pads (these are absorbent and work better than newspaper) or a litter pan lined with artificial turf (to simulate the outdoors).

Do not be hasty in making the decision of the surface and location that you'll want your dog to use. Training a dog to one surface (cement, for instance) and then later deciding that you'd rather have the dog use grass will frustrate and confuse the dog. You are building on the dog's natural instincts, and changing your mind two months later is extremely difficult for both dog and owner.

themselves often. You won't be changing diapers, thankfully, but you will be leading your puppy to his relief area a dozen or more times per day: after he's been playing, after he's eaten, after he's been sleeping, and any other times that he indicates that he needs to "go."

For an eight-week-old puppy, you will need to take him out every hour. That's one very good reason that it's good to have someone at home all day when you first adopt a puppy. The older the puppy, the less frequently he'll need to go out.

Fortunately, once the puppy is around four months old, he'll only need to go out seven or eight times a day. Finally, the normal adult dog will only have to relieve himself three to five times per day.

Housing

Your house-training success will also depend on how much freedom you allow your puppy when he's indoors. You can't expect a puppy to establish a routine if you grant him access to every room of your home. This is akin to taking an excited

The crate may well be the most necessary accessory you buy for your dog, as it can mean a clean lifestyle for you and your dog.

HOUSETRAINING HIGHLIGHTS

Use a crate. Even a puppy will try hard not to soil his bed, and if he does go in his crate, it's an easy-to-clean area and not your best carpet.

- Have a schedule and stick to it. Take your puppy out after meals, after playtime, and whenever he wakes up from a nap.
- Watch your puppy's body language. Circling, sniffing, and squatting are signs he is going to go. Pick him up, and take him outside. Don't try to call him outside. You need to pick him up, with luck, before he goes.
- Use the same door to the outside, and take your puppy to the same area of the yard each time.
- Choose a word or phrase to indicate that you want him to relieve himself. Whatever phrase you're comfortable with, use it. Give lots of praise when he goes.
- Take him out on a lead. This is not playtime. Once he's relieved himself, you can play with him.

SIZE MATTERS

The size of the crate (or alcove) becomes the most critical factor in the house-training equation. The area must be large enough for the puppy to lie down and stretch out as well as stand up without rubbing his head on the top, yet small enough so that he cannot relieve himself at one end and sleep at the other without coming into contact with his droppings. The basis of crate training is that canines are naturally clean animals who do not wish to sleep or eat anywhere near their relief areas.

By providing sleeping and resting quarters that fit the dog, and offering frequent opportunities for him to relieve himself outside his quarters, the puppy quickly learns that the outdoors (or newspaper if you're training him to paper) is the place to go when he needs to urinate or defecate. It also reinforces his innate desire to keep his sleeping quarters clean. This, in turn, helps develop the muscle control that will eventually produce a dog with clean living habits.

child to an amusement park and telling him that the place is all his and that he can do whatever he wants! This would be too much for the child—and the puppy—to handle. It is better to provide the puppy clearly defined areas where he can play, sleep, eat, and share time with his family.

The most sensible choice would be the family room or den (all dogs like dens). Since canines are social creatures, they need to identify with the family (their new pack) and feel a part of the pack right from the start. Hearing your voice, watching you while you're doing things, and smelling you nearby are all positive reinforcers now that he is a member of your pack. The family room, or some other centrally located room, is ideal for providing safety and security for both puppy and owner.

As the crate will become a critical part of your puppy's world, it's ideal to place the crate in this chosen room. Most dogs

Selecting a crate of the proper size for your puppy is not a difficult task. Always select the size that your dog will require as a full-grown adult. Your local pet shop should carry the type of crate you will need.

prefer the wire-type crates, though the fiberglass crates are also very popular. If you have a large-breed puppy and do not wish to crate-train him, you can create a small alcove for the puppy. What you want to do is to create a "den," a place the puppy can call his own. This way, he can be in his own place within the family unit.

The crate or area should be lined with a clean towel. Offer one toy, not more. Do not put food or water in the crate, as eating and drinking will activate his digestive processes and ultimately defeat your purpose as well as make the puppy very uncomfortable as he attempts to "hold it." Once the puppy is reliably house-trained, you can then provide clean water to him at all times.

Another valuable lesson is never to line his sleeping area with newspaper. Remember that most breeders line their whelping pens with newspapers, and this is where the pups first learn to relieve themselves. Once in your home, the puppy will immediately associate newspaper with voiding. Never put newspaper on any floor while house-training, as this will be an open invitation for the puppy to go potty. One of your main goals is not to confuse the puppy. If you're paper-training him, use paper in his designated relief area only. Finally, restrict water intake after evening meals. Offer a few licks at a time; never let a young puppy gulp water after meals.

Benefits of the Crate

Human children must be educated to understand what their parents expect of them and, likewise, puppies (a different species entirely from *Homo sapiens*) must also be taught how to become compatible with human routines and expectations. Thus, you must teach the puppy when it is time to play, eat, sleep, learn, entertain himself, etc. We are teaching the puppy control, helping him to develop a lifestyle that fits in with that of his human family.

WHAT A CRATE PARTY!

The crate is also a fine party tool! Your dog can be on the guest list without being in the way (or begging and bothering all your guests.) The pup in his crate can have a ringside seat at the party and feel a part of the fun, without being underfoot and being fed fatty, sugary treats that will upset his stomach.

Your puppy should always sleep in his crate. He should also learn that there will be times when he is expected to keep away from his bustling family members. He will learn that he should not be underfoot in the morning when his family is preparing for their day (leaving the house to hunt, gather new toys, chase plotting kitties, etc.) as well as other times of excessive activity. His crate is the ideal place to rest and entertain himself in safety and comfort at times like these.

Establishing a Schedule for the Puppy

Consistency and frequency are the preamble to successful house-training. Your pup needs to be led to his relief area every time that he is released from his crate, after meals, after exercise or play sessions, when he first awakens from a nap, etc. For the young pup, 8–10 weeks of age, you will be making the potty walk an hourly event. As the puppy grows, he'll be able to wait for longer periods of time.

Brevity will pay off during your potty trips, or else the pup may learn to linger

and not take care of the business at hand. Stay no more than five minutes, and then return to the house. If he goes during that time, praise lavishly and take him indoors immediately. If he doesn't, but he has an accident when you go back indoors, pick him up immediately, say "No! No!" and return to his relief area. Wait a few minutes, then return to the house again.

Once indoors, put him in his crate until you've had time to clean up his accident. The lesson here is yours: Watch the puppy more closely. Let him back into his designated family area and be more vigilant in looking for his signs that he has to "go." In all likelihood, his accident was a result of your not picking up his signal or waiting too long before offering him the opportunity to relieve himself. Even when your pup has an accident, remain positive. Punishment has no place in house-training. You will not impress the pup by scolding him or hitting him. Such methods are arcane and completely ineffective.

Your puppy should also have regular play and exercise sessions when he's with you or a family member. Exercise for a

CRATE SAFETY

You should crate the puppy each time you leave him by himself in the house. This is for his safety as well as for your own mental well-being. It is obvious that all puppies are chewers and that they don't have good judgment about what they can and can't chew (regardless of how many tasty nylon bones you provide them). They don't know a proper bone from chewy lamp cords or television wires. Chewing into an electrical wire, for example, can be fatal to the puppy, while a shorted wire can start a fire in the house. If the puppy were in his crate, he would not be harming himself or burning down your house!

An uncrated puppy can find all kinds of mischief in an uncharted house. If the puppy chews on the leg of your dining room table when he's alone, you will probably discipline him angrily when you get home. Thus, he makes the association that your coming home means he's going to be punished. (He doesn't recall carving up the furniture and will not associate your anger with anything he did!)

The crate also provides privacy and a door between your puppy and solicitous urchins! If you have a small child in the home who wants to get into the puppy's food bowl every time he eats, feeding the pup in his crate is the answer. The child can't disturb the dog, and the pup will be free to eat in peace. All dogs should eat without interference. The puppy that has to defend his food bowl may become aggressive towards children or other similar "villains."

very young puppy can consist of a short walk around the house or yard. Playing can include fetching games with a large ball or an old sock with a knot tied in the middle (all puppies teethe and need soft things on which to chew). Remember to restrict play periods to indoors within his living area (the family room, for example) until he's completely house-trained. Do not permit the puppy to run amok around the house. After vigorous exercise, your puppy will need to relieve himself.

Do not use the pup's relief area as an alternative playground. The puppy must understand that this area indicates that it's time to relieve himself, not look for a frisbee. Once trained, he'll be able to play indoors and out and still differentiate the times for play versus the times for relief.

Develop a schedule for the puppy that revolves around his crate. Establish regular hours for naps, being alone, playing by himself and just resting, all in his crate. Encourage him to entertain himself while you're busy with your activities. Let him learn that having you near is comforting, but that your main purpose in life is not to provide him with your undivided attention.

Crate training provides safety for you, the puppy, and the home. It also provides the puppy with a feeling of security, and that helps develop a puppy with self-confidence and clean habits. Many breeders will begin crate training before the puppy leaves them, but if your puppy is not familiar with staying in a crate, follow these steps to get him used to the crate.

Six Steps to Successful Crate Training

Remember, one of the most important components in your pup's house-training regimen is control. Regardless of your lifestyle, there will always be occasions when you'll need to have a place where your dog can stay and be happy and safe. Crate

POSITIVE CRATE TRAINING

Never use crate as a place for punishment. It's not like a parent who sends his child to his room for a minor misdemeanor. You want the puppy to associate his special area with positive things, not punishment. Each time you put the puppy in his crate, tell him, "It's crate time!" (or whichever command you choose). Soon, he'll happily run to his crate when he hears you say those words. In the beginning of his training, don't leave him in his crate for prolonged periods of time, except during the night when everyone is sleeping. Make his experience with his crate a pleasant one and, as an adult, he'll love it and willingly stay in it for several hours. There are millions of people who go to work every day and leave their adult dogs crated while they're away. The dogs accept this as their lifestyle and look forward to "crate time."

The crate will become your puppy's own special place, like a doggy bedroom or private sanctuary. Your puppy will retire to his crate for a nap or just when he needs a break from his humans.

training is absolutely the best option for dog owners and their well-trained dogs.

Following are the step-by-step directions to actually training your puppy to accept his crate as his den, a place of security and comfort. Follow each step in order and don't try to rush the final steps. A conscientious approach to training now will result in a happy dog that willingly accepts your lifestyle as his own.

1. Tell the puppy, "It's crate time!" and place him in the crate with a small treat (a piece of cheese or half a biscuit). Let him stay in the crate for five minutes while you are in the same room, then release him and praise lavishly. Never release him when he's fussing. Wait until he's quiet before you let him out.

2. Repeat Step 1 several times a day.

3. The next day, place the puppy in the crate as before. Let him stay there for ten minutes. Do this several times.

4. Continue building time in 5-minute increments until the puppy will stay in his crate for 30 minutes with you in the room. Always take him to his relief area after prolonged periods in his crate.

5. Now go back to the beginning and let puppy stay in his crate for five minutes while you are out of the room.

6. Once again, build crate time in five-minute increments with you out of the room. When the puppy will stay willingly in his crate (he may even fall asleep!) for 30 minutes with you out of the room, he'll be ready to stay in it for several hours at a time.

PUPPY DEVELOPMENT: THE FIRST EIGHT MONTHS

It is helpful for dog owners to understand the basic development of young dogs so that they can apply this information to their training efforts. During the first seven weeks of a puppy's life, his needs are simple. Such basics as food, sleep, and warmth are provided by his dam, who is the source of security and discipline. Puppies during this stage already respond to gentle touching, and they learn from interaction with their littermates. The pup's pack instincts are already developing, and he understands that his dam is the pack leader. Up until the age of seven weeks, when they should be still at the breeder's home, the pups socialize with humans and become increasingly aware of their surroundings.

By the eighth week of age, the puppy needs to begin experiencing the outside world. The pup's brain is fully developed and he's ready to be removed from his dam and siblings. Most behaviorists identify a fear period sometime during the 8th through 16th week, usually lasting 4 weeks. Owners should be gentle and reassuring with pups during this period, as they are increasingly impressionable and need human contact and encouragement.

Obedience training can be instituted around the 13th week, when the puppy begins to become more human than canine. He is experiencing the human world in full force and his socialization has led him to learn about the world's nouns: lots of people, places, and things. The puppy enters adolescence, so you must approach this creature like any other teenager. Be firm and fair, and be consoled by the fact that puppies won't threaten to "hate you for life" if you take away their favorite nylon bone or refuse to drive them to the park. You want to encourage your adolescent puppy, but do not allow him to rule the roost or else your lack of

Puppies are much easier to train when they are less than 16 weeks of age. At about four months of age, their hormones begin to flow, and the restful puppy becomes a restless puppy looking for the friendly scent of the opposite sex.

discipline could spoil your dog for years to come. At this period, until around 16 weeks, the pup's flight instincts become prominent, though this will vary from breed to breed.

By the time your pup reaches the four-month milestone, he will become more dominant and want to sow his proverbial oats. Such behavior accompanies sexual maturity, which is usually reached around this time. Fortunately, you have begun obedience training and the dog will respond to basic commands. Training during this very distracting period is more difficult, and be aware that a second but more brief fear period could occur between the seventh and eighth month.

Having a thorough knowledge of how dogs learn and the methods we'll use in the dog's training will assure a strong foundation for the puppy. Thus, a few guidelines and explanations come first.

1. For a dog to learn a new behavior, he must perform it for 42 consecutive days in a variety of places with heightening distractions. This idea was originally proclaimed by Dr. Ivan Pavlov, the Russian physiologist, as a result of his studies of the learning process.

2. Dr. Edward Thorndike, a noted American psychologist, gave us a

Whether the new behavior is the simple sit command or something more advanced like walking through an agility tunnel, inducing the puppy to obey is the preferred method of positive training that we will pursue.

learning theory that applies equally to dog and man. It states that a behavior that results in a pleasant event tends to be repeated, while a behavior that results in an unpleasant event tends not to be repeated.

3. Harvard professor, Dr. B. F. Skinner, gave us *shaping*, which is the practice of using a reinforcement to effect some change in behavior which is signaled by a stimulus. A positive reinforcement is something the puppy wants, such as a toy or a food treat. In your training method, you will use positive reinforcements to help your puppy master his new behaviors.

For example, telling the dog to "sit" becomes the stimulus, sitting becomes the desired behavior, and the food treat is the positive reinforcement. Alternative terms for positive and negative training methods are "inducive" and "compulsive," respectively.

Inducive methods create a desire in the puppy to do what you tell him to do because you have something he wants (toys, food treats, etc.) Compulsive methods create avoidance in the subject because they're unpleasant ("No!," a sharp jerk on the collar, etc.). Negative methods are not generally used for teaching new behaviors, especially to puppies.

In addition to the inducive method of training, your puppy will also learn three distinct languages. Without even being conscious of it, he'll learn the language of your hands, the language of your feet, and your verbal language. At the conclusion of his training, the puppy will be able to execute his various behaviors simply by watching the movements of your hands and feet and listening to the sounds of your voice.

While all of this may sound a bit complicated at first, it will become familiar and comfortable for you as the training progresses. Soon, you won't even think about all of the information I'm giving you right now. However, it is important that you are aware of how dogs learn and what type of methods we'll be using in the weeks ahead. That way, your puppy will learn rapidly and avoid making mistakes in the process. The result? You'll both be winners!

TRAINING EQUIPMENT

Puppy training requires some basic equipment, which can be purchased at a local pet shop for a reasonable price. First, the puppy will need a collar, which you may already have. You'll also need a leash or, as we will call it, a lead. These two items become important links between you, your puppy, and his schooling. You'll use the collar and leash each time you work with the puppy. Soon, the puppy will begin to associate the collar and lead with you and the fun that lies ahead for him as he works with you.

Next, you'll need food treats, a few of your puppy's favorite toys, a small blanket or cushion upon which he can rest, and a wooden dowel, which he'll learn to retrieve. A six-foot-long, thin nylon line with a clasp at one end and no loop at the other end will be used as a house line for puppies who need a bit more control than most. For example, let's say you have an excitable puppy that races around the house each time you want him to come to you or at times gets so excited that he finds self-control impossible. Having a house line attached to his collar will give you control in managing the puppy.

Dress collars are usually available at your local pet shop.

House Line

You can either purchase or make your own house line. It should be made of lightweight round nylon cording, about six feet long, with a small clasp at one end. Do not have a loop at the other end. Instead, burn the tip of the free end with a match so the nylon threads melt and become sealed, and thus won't unravel. Not all puppies will need to wear a house line. Its purpose is to give you control over the puppy as he plays freely in the house

No two puppies learn in the exact same way. Owners must commit to understanding the way dogs think before they can successfully train puppies to obey commands.

COLLARS & LEASHES OR LEADS

A simple nylon buckle collar is best for a puppy. Check chains or choke chains are inappropriate for puppies because they are made of metal links, which can cause severe damage to the neck and throat if used incorrectly by mistake. Prong or spike collars are also inappropriate and should only be used by knowledgeable handlers on adult dogs that absolutely resist all other forms of control.

The leash or lead should be six feet long and made of cotton webbing, nylon, or leather. Cotton webbing is the softest and easiest to use. Nylon can be sharp along the edges and burn or cut your skin if it slips through your hands when the puppy darts away from you. Leather is the ideal material for a training lead, but it can be expensive. However, if cared for, it will last for years and become softer with use like a good leather glove.

A chain lead is out of the question for training. The metal links will be too rough on your hands and cause you great discomfort whenever the puppy pulls on the lead. In addition, it will rattle each time it moves, which will prove disruptive to the dog's learning process.

Finally, a flexible lead should not be used for training. I discourage people from ever using one with a puppy until the puppy has successfully learned to walk at the heel position without pulling. Flexible leads allow the dog to walk out 10 to 15 feet ahead of you and pull hard as if he were a sled dog and you were a sled! Flexible leads also are not recommended for large-breed dogs. Bad habits that are set early in the puppy's life will be extremely difficult to alter as he gets older, so avoid these leads until the puppy is well trained and can walk politely on-lead.

Simple nylon collars and leads are best for puppy training.

GROOM HIM INTO CALMNESS

Teach your puppy enjoy being groomed. It doesn't matter whether he's a long-coated breed or a short-coated one, he will still need grooming from time to time throughout his life. Take the process slowly and in small steps.

Brush one side a day and reward him with a biscuit as soon as you finish. Examine only one ear and two feet the first day. Repeat the process on the other side of the dog the following day. Look in his mouth and examine his teeth. Be calm and deliberate, and speak in a soothing voice to let him know he's a good boy for allowing you to groom him. "Oh, what a good dog you are! How handsome!" Again, reward the final exam with a biscuit and more praise. Eventually, he'll settle down and enjoy the whole ritual because it gets him lots of positive attention from you. Be patient and never lose your temper with the puppy.

with you. He should never be allowed to wear the house line when you are not with him or when he's in his crate.

If you've ever tried to catch a whirling puppy as he races around the house in a frantic game of "catch-me-if-you-can," then you know how frustrating it can be. Usually you end up chasing the pup and getting angry because he seems totally oblivious to the fact that you want him to stop. Thus, your frustration only serves to excite the puppy even more, and the two of you end up in an impossible situation that will surely happen again and again.

The house line allows you to step on or grab the line as the pup races past you. This action demonstrates to the puppy that he must slow down and respond to your call to come. Since you were able to catch him with the help of the house line, you can praise him lavishly for coming to you so willingly—even though you made it happen! Thus, he learns to respond correctly and promptly in the future rather than to embark on another chase game.

You can also initiate a game of "gotcha," where you call the puppy, grab his collar, hold for just a moment, then

Just like treats, toys can be used as rewards during training. Remove the special toy after the day's lessons have been completed.

Toys and Dowel

Toys are used for rewards just as food treats are used. If, for example, you tell the puppy to sit and he obeys, you can change the pace of training occasionally by throwing him a toy that had been previously hidden in your pocket instead of offering a food treat. When you toss the toy out in front of the dog, tell him to "Go get it!" He'll race out to fetch it and you can stop the training momentarily to have a little play session. This will break up the routine of training and give the puppy an unexpected surprise in the middle of a lesson. Once you've had a short play session, remove the toy, put it away, and resume normal training.

A dowel will be used to teach the puppy to retrieve. Fetching items is one of the most useful behaviors you can teach your dog and it's easy for him to learn if the lessons are begun in the form of play when he's a puppy. The dowel should be six or seven inches long and have a diameter that is appropriate to the size of the puppy's mouth. For example, a one-quarter-inch dowel is fine for a toy breed, whereas a large-breed puppy should have a dowel with a one-half-inch or five-eighth-inch diameter.

Blanket or Cushion

As you begin to develop a line of communication with your puppy and he begins to learn his new behaviors, you'll

release the puppy to go back to playing or whatever he was doing. This teaches the puppy that the fun doesn't end when you call him. Many dogs become reluctant to obey the "come" command because it means the end of fun. Also, many dogs will obey the command, but then run off again before they can be leashed. Get your puppy used to someone holding his collar. Use the house line, if you must, to encourage him to come.

Since any line attached to the puppy can be a potential danger if it catches on a piece of furniture or in a doorway, the house line must only be used when somebody is with the dog. Never leave any line on your puppy when he's alone or in his crate.

Train your puppy to know where his bed is and when he should use it. You should have acquired a suitable bed or cushion and a crate before you bring the puppy home.

want to teach him that there are times when he must go away from you and rest quietly on his own bed. The blanket or cushion will serve as his target place for resting when this occurs.

I don't recommend using carpet squares for this purpose because they are stiff and impossible to fold into small sizes for carrying to various places that you may go with your dog. A blanket or small cushion can be rolled up and tucked under your arm whenever the need for moving it arises.

Food Treats

Food in training is used for teaching new behaviors and sometimes for solving performance problems in previously trained dogs. The latter aspect will not concern us here because puppies are far too young to develop performance problems such as those that might be seen in competition training with adult dogs.

Food used in puppy training makes the learning so much more exciting and successful. After all, Dr. Thorndike's theory of a behavior that results in a pleasant event proves correct when applied to puppies.

The kind of food used for treats is important. Dry dog biscuits are not suitable for puppy training. If you tell a puppy to sit and he complies, and then you give him a dry dog biscuit, it will take him too long to chew up the biscuit before he can swallow it. The time that elapses between the actual sit and the swallowing of the treat is so long that the puppy makes no connection between the sit and the reward.

There are some human foods that usually prove ideal for dog training because they're nutritious, good-smelling, soft, and easily swallowed. These include small slices of hotdog, small cubes of cheddar cheese, little pieces of cooked chicken, beef, or turkey, and small bits of mildly flavored sausage.

Often, I'm asked if using food in training will teach the dog to beg at the table. The answer is *no*! The only way to teach to beg at the table is to offer him food from the table. Your training will be all over the house and outside, and the treats will always come from his school bag. He will make no connection between his treat bag and the food that's on your plate at the table, providing that you never feed him while you're at the table.

Usually, giving a variety of treats while training will be better for the puppy than offering single items such as cheese. Too much of anything can give the puppy an upset stomach. Also, be sure to figure in the nutritional and caloric value of his treats when feeding his regular meals or you'll end up with a very fat—albeit well-educated—dog. Rest assured, we will eliminate the use of food in training by the end of this course, and the puppy will learn to obey for praise alone. Remember,

TREATS IN HIS SCHOOL BAG

Before you begin training, offer your puppy a variety of treats to find out exactly what he likes. Avoid those in which he shows no interest and prepare a variety of treats that he does like. Place them in a small plastic bag that can be stored in the refrigerator. This bag then becomes his school bag and he'll quickly learn that his special treat bag lives in that big box in your kitchen. He may even anticipate a treat by going to the refrigerator from time to time and sitting quite still in the hope that you'll reach in and produce a treat! If he does, you can be sure that you've got a smart little puppy on your hands and he's learned that going to school produces treats from his school bag!

we use food only to teach new behaviors. We don't want to spend the rest of our lives walking around with bags of treats in our pockets!

Skinner's theory of operant conditioning works beautifully in dog training. Because we use food in training, the command "Sit" stimulates the dog to sit and be instantly rewarded with a treat and praise. Eventually, the food is stopped but the praise continues. The dog is now conditioned to obey the sit command

Food rewards are the best rewards during puppy training. Use a treat that is small, soft, and easily swallowed, like soft cheese or a piece of cooked meat. Hard cookies that require a lot of chewing are distracting for training purposes.

solely for the forthcoming praise. That's operant conditioning in action.

PRAISE

When you're working with a dog, a casual word of praise for a job well done is not enough. In fact, it's usually meaningless. Throughout this book, you will see such phrases as "praise lavishly," "praise generously," "praise your dog simultaneously as you give him the treat," etc. The kind of praise your dog needs in these learning situations is *enthusiastic* praise. Clap your hands and applaud your dog. Laugh and tell him what a good puppy he is. Let him know that whatever he just did pleases you immensely. Don't be shy. Let your pride in his learning shine through so that he'll know how special he is. Your enthusiastic praise will pay off quickly in creating an enthusiastic student.

THE PACK AND THE LEADER

These are two outdated terms. Yes, dogs are social animals, and yes, they descended from wolves, who do travel in packs. Beyond that, dogs have been domesticated for so long that the idea that they follow any kind of pack structure, with the human as the "alpha" is not true. Yes, dogs need structure, but the type of structure differs from family to family. As a family member, your puppy will soon learn the family rules, and be content to follow them.

Some people point to the litter box and say that the dam is the "leader" of the pack that comprises mother and pups. She does keep her pups safe, but that's her job, and of course she's the leader. Puppies are pretty helpless when born and need to follow their mother's lead to stay safe and healthy.

Once a puppy joins your family, it is up to you to keep him safe and healthy and to help him learn the rules of the household, but beyond that, your relationship should be more of a partnership than that of dominant over submissive.

Even within the same breed, puppies can have different personalities, just as people do. One puppy may be very outgoing, willing to try anything, and seemingly fearless. Another puppy may be a bit shy and need gentle handling when facing something new. Temperament testing by the breeder may help you to know which type of personality you will be getting. Depending on your lifestyle, you might want a quieter, less-curious dog, or you might want the more outgoing personality. Neither is wrong, just different. An outgoing dog may learn a bit faster because nothing is scaring him. With a shyer dog, you need to be patient and upbeat and assure him that a stranger or a loud noise is normal and nothing to be afraid of. All puppies need to experience different things as they grow so they are confident adults.

Dogs generally appreciate structure in their lives, but what that structure looks like is entirely up to you. Let's start with feeding your dog. Some people will tell you to always feed your dog after you've eaten to show him you're the leader. That's not necessary. You're not sharing a bowl, with you taking your share first. The dog knows you're the one providing the food, and when you feed the dog is entirely up to you. If you feed your dog before your own meal, he will be full, and less likely to beg at the table (to stop that, don't ever start with any food from the table). Sometimes, I feed my dogs first, sometimes, last. I do ask my bouncier dog to "wait" before setting down his bowl, and many people want their dogs to sit before they place the bowl. Both of these things help eliminate spilled kibble from a dog lunging at the dish, but it's your choice.

Another behavior that is often stressed is to never let your dog precede you through a doorway. That depends. Yes, it's a very good rule to make sure your dog doesn't dart out into traffic, but teaching a "wait" or a "stay" command can keep your dog where you want him. If, for whatever reason, you want your dog to go ahead of you out the door or down the stairs, tell him, "Okay," or whatever word you choose to release your dog.

Making your dog wait before leaping from a car is almost more important, because with the car, you're more likely to be near a busy road or in a busy parking lot. Start young. Also, dogs are situational learners. "Wait" or "stay" taught in the living room is not the same as those commands in a car. Give lots of praise and practice somewhere safe. If you have a garage, practice there. Just don't turn on the car.

Play sessions are just that. Play. Some dogs love tug-of-war games, and no, you don't always have to win. If your dog is very strong, and you want to moderate his pulling, fine, but otherwise, there's no reason you can't let your puppy win. It's supposed to be fun. Let the puppy win and enjoy watching him race around with his prize. You can always stop a play session, but you don't always have to win.

Many people think you shouldn't let your dog sleep with you in your bed, but there's no reason you can't let a clean, calm dog sleep with you. If you're worried that he will think it's his bed alone, only let him up on the bed when you invite him; don't let him just jump up. It can be a comfort to have a dog to snuggle, and with one of my dogs, she only wants to sleep with us during thunderstorms and that's fine.

Whether your dog is allowed on any furniture or not, remember that puppies learn quickly. If you don't want the adult dog to sleep with you or get on the sofa, then don't start when he's a puppy. It's easier to never start a habit than to try to break it. Your dog will be just as happy sleeping in his crate if it's in your room, and a crate can make a wonderful bedside table.

Puppies love to investigate and chew everything, some of which can be dangerous or deadly, such as electrical wires and TV cords. Crate training prevents all these things from happening and allows you and your puppy to enjoy life with you as the boss. Remember that it's as much of an obligation to provide the puppy with leadership as it is to feed him properly and give him a safe environment in which to live.

Your Relationship with the Shy Puppy

How can you help the submissive puppy gain self-confidence and overcome his shyness? There are a number of ways to do this that require little time but will prove helpful if done regularly. First, never pet or caress the dog when he shows signs of stress or shyness. This action will only serve to reinforce his belief that he should be afraid or that, by being afraid and acting fearful, he can get lots of attention from you. If the dog expresses concern about an event or a place that he finds worrisome, simply say something like, "Oh, that's just a strange noise (or a man walking down the street or whatever)." Act very casual about the situation and redirect the puppy's attention to something pleasant, such as taking a walk or chasing a ball or some other game he enjoys. The bottom line here: Never reinforce a behavior that you don't want repeated, and always exhibit a casual, happy attitude about whatever concerns the puppy.

Spend a few minutes each day grooming the dog. Brush his coat, examine his feet, look in his ears, check his teeth. All the while you're doing this, tell him what a good dog he is and how pretty he is. "Oh, what pretty feet you have. Look at these nice white teeth. You're so handsome and such a good dog!"

He will soon learn to love the special grooming times he has with you because they are always pleasant experiences and leave him feeling good about himself. A dog biscuit when the grooming time is over will be the perfect end to a nice little ritual that you can share together.

Feed your puppy at the same time that you eat. Don't stress waiting in the doorway if he's too upset over seeing you go ahead without him. Once he builds his self-confidence, he can learn to wait his turn in doorways and automobiles.

Designate a special chair for him near where you sit to read, write, or watch television. You can cover the chair with a special towel or old sheet that will protect your furniture while it lets the dog know the chair is his to use. You can even keep a few chew toys on the chair to reinforce the idea that the chair is part of his territory.

Give the puppy as many new life experiences as you possibly can so that he learns that the two of you will go many places and do many things together, and that you, his leader, will assure his comfort and safety in all situations. That's called trust, and it's an important element in any relationship. In a future lesson, you will be assigned several new things for you to do with your puppy to build his confidence.

THINGS TO DO
BEFORE OBEDIENCE LESSONS

- Obtain training equipment.
- Test puppy for his food preferences.
- Test puppy for outgoing or shy temperament.
- Begin teaching grooming without resistance.
- Begin crate training.

Before you begin teaching your dog, think about clicker training. The training methods that follow are good ones, and for a puppy learning the basics, they are fine, but for more training, clicker training may work better. You can use clicker training to work at a distance from your dog, and you don't need to depend on the collar or lead. Clickers are tiny devices that make a sound when the metal is bent, like an old cricket toy. The sound the clicker makes acts as a marker that a particular action is correct. Then a reward follows. You don't have to use a clicker with your dog; you can choose a word as your marker. The advantage to the clicker is that it is the same sound every time; there's no vocal inflection. If you decide you want to use a word, use the same word every time. Don't say "good" and then switch to "yes."

We talk to our dogs all the time, but the sound of the clicker is unique and is only heard when your dog has done the right thing. You can buy clickers in many pet-supply stores, or just search online. Some books on clicker training come with a clicker.

The first step in clicker training is to "charge the clicker." This is teaching your dog that when he hears the clicker, he's going to get a reward. To charge the clicker, click and treat ten to twelve times in a row. Once your dog understands that the sound means good things, you can start to train.

There are three ways to use clicker training. The easiest to understand is luring. This is what's used for most of the behaviors that follow. You use your food reward to guide the dog into whatever behavior you want, then click and give him the food. For example, using a bit of food and gradually moving it back over the dog's head, you can lure him into a sit. Click and treat. Eventually, you can name the behavior, and when your dog hears the command to sit, he will do it without the lure, and you can again click and treat.

With shaping, you work on a behavior in increments. For teaching your dog to go to a specific spot when you need the dog to be out of the way, or when someone comes to the door, try this method. Use a small mat or rug to mark the spot. Click

You can't teach a dog anything unless the dog gives you his undivided attention. Understand that dogs don't speak our language, but they can associate certain sounds with certain behaviors.

"Do you want to go to school?" Reinforce to your puppy that "school" equates to good times with his mistress.

and treat when the dog walks over the mat. Then, when the dog actually stops on the mat, click for that, and not for just walking across the mat. If the dog sits, or lies down, that action gets clicked and treated. Gradually, when the command to "place" or "go to your mat" is given, the dog will head for his spot. You can try this, or follow the guidelines further on in this book.

Capturing is when you see your dog do something you want him to do, and you click and treat. You may see that your dog likes to curl up for a nap in a particular spot. So, you put a rug or blanket there. When you see your dog curling up there, you click and treat. Or, maybe you think it would be fun to be able to ask your dog

if he was sleepy and have him yawn as a response. Every time your dog yawns, click and treat. Eventually, you can name the behavior, and your dog will respond on cue.

Clicker training takes patience, but the more you use it, the faster your dog will catch on to the process. Many dogs will begin offering all the behaviors they know, hoping to get that reward. When that light bulb goes off for your dog, and he understands the game, you can teach him just about anything, and you'll both love the process. It will be a game for you both.

Before a dog can learn anything, he must learn to pay attention. After all, you can't teach him something if he's busy watching someone or something else. You, in turn, need to realize that dogs don't understand or speak our verbal language. They can and do, however, learn the meaning of certain sounds, providing that a particular sound is always matched with a particular behavior.

The spoken word "sit" to the dog soon translates to his placing his rump on the floor in a sitting position when the command is accompanied by positive reinforcement such as a food treat. Therefore, when training a dog, the key to success in teaching any behavior is being consistent in the use of command words, using a pleasant tone of voice to keep the dog attentive, and presenting the treat and verbal praise simultaneously as soon as the dog executes the desired behavior.

To start any lesson, you'll need your puppy. Call him, using a happy, excited voice. When he comes, either mark with a clicker, or just use enthusiastic praise. You'll want to give praise anyway. Pet him and give him several small training treats. Use this method whenever you want your puppy to come; it doesn't have to be for a lesson. Call him to eat, even if he's already

After your puppy has executed the sit command a few times, each time receiving praise and a tidbit, call it a day! Do not make sessions overly long or monotonous, lest your puppy loseth heart!

Before you begin training, call your pup over in a happy and excited voice, and use this same enthusiastic tone whenever you want him to come.

on the way. Call him for the game of "gotcha," then let him return to whatever he was doing. Call him for a walk or a ride if he enjoys those things. Just remember, NEVER call your puppy to punish him or for something he dislikes. If you want to cut his nails, and he hates that, go and get him; don't call him to you.

As your puppy matures, he will learn certain words and phrases that mean something pleasant is going to happen. If you want to name your training sessions, go ahead. Say, "school," or "lesson time." My own dogs know that if I get my clicker, it means treats. Keep lessons short and fun, and your dog will enjoy learning as much as you enjoy teaching him.

PRACTICE

Practice is the secret ingredient in successful dog training, just as it is for humans who are working to perfect a skill or craft. The key for dogs, however, is never to practice too much or for too long

THE SPOON TRICK

Occasionally, a puppy might have a habit of taking treats as if he were a piranha! He grabs the food and the fingers holding it without realizing that he's biting the owner's fingers as well as the treat. Trying to slow him down so he takes the food treat in a gentle way is impossible.

If this happens to you, and your dog grabs at the food instead of taking it gently, I have a trick for you to use. Employing this trick for a week usually cures the most voracious treat-grabber.

Take a large soup spoon and place the bowl of the spoon in your right hand. Place a good-sized food treat in the spoon at the very tip. Hold the edge of the treat down in the spoon with your thumb. Be sure your index finger is against the back of the spoon and away from the spoon's tip.

Tell the dog to sit. When he does, say, "Easy, take it easy." Present the treat on the spoon as his reward. As the dog goes to grab the treat, his bottom teeth will come into contact with the metal spoon's underside and he'll not be able to grab the food so readily. Instantly, he'll open his mouth again and attempt to take the food from the spoon, but this time he'll be more gentle when he does. Tell him he's a good boy, and release the food as he takes it.

Do not hold the spoon at the end of the handle. This will seem to the dog that the spoon is an appendage to your hand. We want the dog to think that the bowl of the spoon is part of your hand and, being metal, it is very uncomfortable to bite down on. However, he'll quickly learn that taking the food with a soft mouth produces the treat and that the hard metal feel against his teeth is not a problem as long as he takes the food gently.

"Good boy" (and good treat) at the same time. Who wouldn't sit on command?

seconds at a time will teach the puppy to hate sitting. "Sit, get up. Sit, get up. Sit, get up." See what I mean? Let your puppy do a few sits, followed by the appropriate treat and praise, and then quit. Leave the practice session with the puppy wishing you'd do it just one more time for one more treat! That way, he'll be anxious to get back to showing you how quickly he can obey when you practice next time.

As time passes and the puppy develops a whole range of new behaviors, you'll need more than five minutes to practice. By then, however, he'll have so many things he can do that he'll never get bored with repetitive behaviors. Remember also that you and your puppy are learning together and you want to make the process pleasant for both of you. Only by associating learning with treats, praise, and doing good things together will the dog develop a strong bond of devotion to you.

Be patient, pleasant and persistent in your teaching. Practice several times a day for short periods. Never practice if you're feeling ill, upset, or impatient. Wait until you're in a positive frame of mind and then let the excitement of working with your new friend create a winning atmosphere. Dogs learn with positive reinforcement and frequency, so practice every day.

at any one time. Boring the puppy with repeated commands and behaviors will make him avoid you and his lessons.

For the first few weeks of training, practice no more than 3 to 5 minutes every 24 hours and no more than 30 seconds at any one time. Just think about it for a moment and you'll understand: If you teach the puppy to sit on command, practicing sitting for more than 30

After being trained to sit indoors, the same process should be used for practicing the lesson outdoors. Don't forget the treat—liver smells even better outside!

TOY-DOG FACTOR: SIT

Sometimes when training a toy-breed puppy, you may encounter a handling problem because of it's tiny size. As you raise your food hand up over the puppy's head, he'll begin to back up instead of sit. He's just trying to keep an eye on the food and needs a little help to understand what you want him to do. This problem is easily solved within a few repetitions of the sit exercise.

Keep your right hand with the food in front of the puppy's nose. Place your open left hand low and behind the puppy so the palm of your hand faces the puppy's rear end and your fingers point toward the floor. As the puppy backs up, he'll back into the palm of your hand and, when he feels the contact, he'll slide down into a sit position. At that point, release the treat and praise lavishly. A few times of allowing him to back up into your open left hand and he'll get the idea that "sit" means to put his rear on the floor.

REWARD AND PRAISE SIMULTANEOUSLY

We will use tasty treats in teaching the puppy all new behaviors. However, we will wean him off the food as soon as possible and before the conclusion of this course. In order to be successful at the weaning process when the time comes, it is absolutely essential that you praise the dog and give him the food treat simultaneously from the beginning of his training. Praise as well as petting. This pairing of food and praise will eventually have the puppy believing he's received a treat for obeying a command when he's only received verbal praise.

In fact, once conditioned to the lessons, he may even salivate whenever he's rewarded verbally for complying with a command. In his mind, he relates food with praise and, when he gets praise, it reminds him of the food treats he's received in the past. (Remember Dr. Pavlov's dogs who salivated when they

A smart dog should be able to identify about six of his favorite toys and bring them to you when he hears you call out their names.

Part of grooming involves inspecting the ears and eyes. Accustoming the pup to this type of handling is useful for trips to the vet, examinations by a show judge, as well as his regular grooming sessions.

heard the dinner bell ring?) Throughout his life, you'll give the dog commands and, providing he was trained properly with simultaneous food and praise, he'll obey reliably. The trick here is always to pair food and praise together, never in sequence to each other.

TEACH "SIT"

With the collar and lead attached to the puppy, hold two food treats in your right hand and the lead in your left hand. Place your food hand at the dog's nose and allow him to nibble one treat. Keep your food hand at the dog's nose and do not move it away from his mouth.

Hold onto the other treat so you can reward him at the conclusion of the exercise. Now say "Sit" and slowly raise your food hand from in front of the dog's nose up over his head so he's looking at the ceiling. As the dog turns his head upward, his knees will automatically bend, which will help him balance himself. As his knees bend, he'll assume a sit position. As soon as he does, release the food and praise him simultaneously. Be sure to praise with great enthusiasm so that he knows he's done something special to please you. Just saying "Good boy" isn't enough when teaching a new behavior.

TEACH "STAND"

Why would you want to teach your dog to stand? There are many occasions when standing is preferable to sitting or lying

▲ When teaching stand, keep your food hand below the pup's eye level. Sometimes it is more difficult to teach a puppy to stand, so you may have to lift the pup from his sitting position a few times until he gets the idea.

▲ Release the treat when the pup is on all fours. Repeat the exercise a few times, but don't allow the dog to become bored with the repetition.

FETCH FOR FUN

Keep in mind that fetching should be a fun activity for young puppies. You won't want to get serious about retrieving until the dog starts to mature. However, even before this course is through, we'll give you some more instruction in teaching retrieving. Some owners forget that puppies are immature and need time to be young, happy, and silly just as children do. There is plenty of time later for the dog to learn about the responsibilities of a serious role in your relationship. So, for now, enjoy the puppy and his activities, use your house line for control and never lose your temper. Keep it happy!

down. Let's say, for example, that you're walking your dog late at night in the pouring rain. When you come to a curb and you're forced to wait for a car to pass in front of you, the dog would normally sit down. That would mean the poor dog has to sit in a muddy puddle, become wet and dirty, and then need a bath when you get home.

Another example is when you bring your dog to the veterinarian for a check-up. The vet may want your dog to stand on the examining table for inspection. The dog that has been trained to stand on command will have no hesitation in obeying the stand command, whereas the dog that has not been trained will become stressed when he's held in a standing position on the slippery table.

Grooming your dog will be accomplished easily when the dog stands and stays on command. If your dog is groomed by a professional, the groomer will not have time to coax him into standing still for grooming. A dog such as a poodle, terrier, or another high-maintenance coated breed must learn right from puppyhood that being groomed is a frequent activity that he must endure with tolerance.

Likewise, dogs that are being trained for showing will need to know how to stand still for an extended period of time. The handler will be required to "stand" or "stack" the dog so that the judge can inspect him properly and thoroughly.

To teach the stand, we use food in the right hand with the lead in the left hand. Tell the puppy to sit, and quickly go stand beside the puppy so that he's on your left side. Now place your food hand at the dog's nose. Hold the treat with the palm of your hand facing the ceiling. Drop your hand slightly below the dog's eye level so he can see the treat in your hand.

As soon as the puppy sees the food in your hand, slowly move your food hand forward about three or four inches as you say "Stand." The puppy will reach his head forward to get the food and then, as your hand moves further forward, he'll stand up to follow the treat. As soon as the puppy is standing on all four feet, stop moving your hand, release the food and praise lavishly.

Do not put any pressure on the lead in your left hand in order to help the puppy stand. If you do, the puppy will resist you, and, in doing so, he'll pull back away from you and remain seated instead of standing. Use only your food hand to get the dog into the stand position. Remember, the food hand is slow and deliberate, and the left hand is still and not attempting to guide the dog in any way. If you have trouble remembering not to pull forward with the lead, just drop the lead and work with your food hand only. Practice in short periods of

Using food to teach your puppy to stand is the most effective method used by trainers.

time, with enthusiasm and treats. Always end on a happy note so that you'll both be anxious to do it again soon.

So far, your puppy has been introduced to two new words this week: "sit" and "stand." Now let's add another word to his repertoire.

NAMING FAVORITE TOYS

During the first week of training, we begin to develop your dog's vocabulary so that, by the end of the eight weeks, he'll be able to identify at least half a dozen toys by name and bring them to you. Remember, the more you help the dog to learn while he's young, the more he can learn for the rest of his life.

Here are a few tips to help you and the puppy make this project easy. First, figure out a name for the dog's favorite toy. The name of the toy should end in the sound of "ee." For example, if the toy is a tennis ball, give it a name like "bouncy" or "tenney." When you tell the puppy to find his "bouncy," the word will incite his curiosity and interest more than the word "ball." Just saying the word "ball" out loud and comparing it with the sound of the word "bouncy" makes it clear that "bouncy" is a more exciting sound than "ball."

Knotted nylon rope toys are very safe for puppies (as long as the knots stay tied). Some are even flavored to further capture the pup's attention.

When you begin teaching the puppy to find his toy by its name, pick up the toy and wiggle it on the ground in front of the dog. Bringing it to life for the puppy will make him more interested in grabbing it than if the toy lay dormant on the floor. Remember, dogs are predators and the chase instinct is a genetic factor. Consequently, you'll never have to teach him to be interested in things that move.

Spend this first week concentrating on one toy and its new name. Say the name hundreds of times so the puppy is flooded with the sound of the name that you've chosen. Each week, introduce a new toy and a new name. By the time this course is finished, your puppy will be able to identify and retrieve six or seven toys.

RETRIEVING TOYS

When the puppy picks up the toy, try to get him to bring it to you. You can even introduce the word "fetch" as he puts the toy in his mouth. That way, in a later week when you begin serious retrieving, he'll be accustomed to fetching. Make sure that, when the puppy brings the toy to you, you take it from him before he drops it on the floor. You want the dog to deliver the object to your hand rather than to drop it near you. Some puppies fetch the toy but then proceed to race around in circles just beyond the owner's reach rather than bring the toy to the person. If this happens with your puppy, use a house line so you can catch him and pull him in to you without your having to make it a chase game.

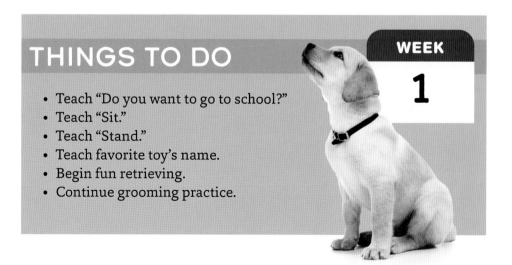

THINGS TO DO

WEEK 1

- Teach "Do you want to go to school?"
- Teach "Sit."
- Teach "Stand."
- Teach favorite toy's name.
- Begin fun retrieving.
- Continue grooming practice.

Puppy Training
The Second Week

This week, we're going to take the first two behaviors that the puppy learned and add to them to create brand-new exercises. These are extremely important because they are what we refer to as control exercises. You'll need to have control of your dog throughout his life, whether he's wearing his collar and lead or not.

The stay exercise will give you that control while it provides a large measure of safety and security for your dog. It is an extremely important behavior that has saved a dog's life on many occasions! To the dog, "Stay" means, "Stop where you are. I'm going to leave you, but I will come right back." Later in this course, we'll teach the wait command, which is a variation of the stay.

In addition to the stay exercises, we'll break out of the cocoon of home and introduce the puppy to the big, busy world outside. It's called socialization, and it's lots of fun for puppy and owner. We'll also address feeding methods and puppy mouthing as well as chewing on forbidden things. Combined with what we taught

the first week, you can see that this will be a busy week.

TEACH "SIT-STAY"

Begin with the dog sitting on your left side, with the lead in your left hand and several treats in your right hand. Place your food hand at the dog's nose, say, "Stay," and step out on your right foot to pivot directly in front of the dog. Keep your feet together and up close, toe to toe with the dog's front feet. Keep your food hand still in front of the dog's nose and allow him to lick or nibble the treat if he chooses. This will help him focus on the right hand, which will eventually become the signal to stay when you leave him. Getting him accustomed to staying and concentrating on the treat allows you to move while he maintains that stay position.

As you stand in front of the dog, keep his nose pointed upward so he maintains a sitting position. Allowing him to drop his head will encourage him to get up and thereby break the sit. Your goal here is to help the dog do the right things as he

A well-trained puppy will stay on command, even without treats!

learns what stay means. Your food treat and praise will demonstrate to him that sitting and waiting while you move away and come back is the behavior you want. Help the puppy be right, and he'll learn the lesson quickly.

While you're out in front of the pup, count to five and then, keeping your food

The sit-stay command is the natural extension of the sit command (and even easier than the sit command). Keep the puppy calm and focused, and the stay command will be as easy as doing nothing at all!

hand still at his nose, return to stand beside the puppy again. Immediately release the food and praise lavishly so he knows that staying was good.

Within a day or so, you can increase the count to 15 and by the end of the week, the puppy should be able to sit and stay to a count of 30. Building up the amount of time that he stays is important because, as he grows, there will be many times when you must leave him for several minutes. He must not move during those times.

It's okay if the puppy nibbles the entire treat while you're standing in front of him. Providing you had several pieces of food in your hand when you began, you'll still have a piece or two left for the final reward when

▲ When in front of the puppy, let him smell the food as he stays for the desired amount of time.

you get back to his side. Be sure that you end the exercise only after returning to his side. Never finish the exercise while you're in front of him.

Regardless of which command you're teaching, a treat is a good thing. The sit and the sit-stay can be accomplished with a consistent command, a proper stance, and a tasty morsel to convince your puppy that your way is the only way.

TEACH "STAND-STAY"

The stand-stay is taught in exactly the same way as the sit-stay except that the puppy is in a standing position rather than a sitting position. Begin with the puppy sitting on your left side, the lead in your left hand and several pieces of food in your right hand. Place your food hand at the dog's nose with the palm facing upward toward the ceiling and slightly below the dog's eye level. Say, "Stand," and move your food hand slowly forward a few inches until the dog stands to follow the food. As soon as the dog is in a standing position, say, "Stay," keep the dog's nose pointing downward, and step out on your right foot to pivot directly in front of the dog. Keep your feet together and up close, toe to toe

▲ Start the sit-stay exercise in front of the puppy, showing him the treat.

▲ If he nibbles the entire treat while you're standing in front of him, be sure to have another treat to give him at the end of the exercise, with you at his side.

▲ Keep him focused on the treat as you move your position to his side.

▲ While rewarding the puppy by releasing the food, praise him lavishly.

with the dog's front feet. Keep your food hand still in front of the dog's nose with his head pointing downward. Allow him to lick or nibble the treat if he chooses. If you raise your hand even an inch or so, the puppy will raise his head to follow the food, thereby causing him to sit.

As you stand in front of the puppy, count to five and then, without moving that food hand, return to the puppy's side. When you get there, give him the treat and praise generously while he's standing beside you. This is the stand-stay, so he must be rewarded while he's still holding that position, not the sit. As with the sit-stay, increase the length of time for which you have him maintain the stand-stay over the coming week. First, move the count up to 15 and finally to 30, with you always helping him to be right as he learns. Lest you think standing for 30 seconds is a long time, remember that being professionally groomed or inspected by the vet or show judge will require him to stand still for a lot longer than 30 seconds, and these are things that he will encounter for the rest of his life!

One final reminder: Don't nag the dog with a constant stream of "stays." Say it once and help him maintain his focus on the lesson at hand by keeping the food at his nose and offering an occasional, softly spoken, "Good stay."

SOCIALIZATION

Let's get out and meet the world this week. What an exciting time it is for your little fellow, and so much fun is ahead for you both! As we mentioned earlier, this

QUIT YOUR JABBERING

Teaching the puppy to obey commands by giving the command only once is important. You don't want to offer a constant stream of jabbering "stay, stay, stay...," etc. This will quickly bore the puppy and cause him to ignore you. Say, "Stay," once and then proceed with leaving him. If, at any time when you're in front of him, you suspect he's about to lie down or get up, you can stop the mistake from happening by repeating the word "stay" once more to reinforce the command. That way, the command will become more meaningful to him.

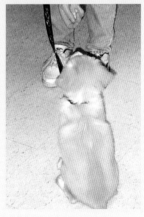

◀ With the treat at his nose, the pup stays focused and still in the sit position.

▲ In the stand-stay, hold the treat so that the dog is looking downward. If the pup has to look up at the treat, he will be tempted to sit down.

WHO'S AT FAULT?

It's important to know that when the puppy makes a mistake in a lesson, chances are it was caused by a handling error. You might have moved your hand inadvertently, stepped out in the wrong direction or stood up when you should have bent over, etc. Teaching yourself to use your entire body correctly to help the dog learn is the other half of the dog training process. That's why I give you such specific instructions for seemingly small moves. Your correct handling and movement will help the dog succeed.

critical age for puppies lasts such a short time and it is so important to the puppy's personality for the rest of his life that we must take it very seriously. We only have a few precious weeks in which to mold this puppy into the dog we'll want to live with for the rest of his life.

No doubt you probably began socializing the puppy before you even realized you were doing it. When you first brought him home, you probably invited friends and neighbors to come meet your new friend. That was your first act of teaching the puppy to accept and enjoy people other than his new family members who live in his home.

Now, this week, we'll take that same concept and move it beyond the home. Take your puppy for a walk to meet your neighbors and their pets and children. Just be aware that not all children or other pets will be kind, gentle, and friendly. Try to determine which ones

are the unfriendly ones before you get involved and avoid them. Introduce your puppy to children by teaching them how to approach the puppy and how to pet him from under the chin and on the

Everyone will be pleased to meet your well-socialized and well-behaved puppy, and vice versa!

Don't be a pushover. At least make the puppy wait for a count of five before moving to his side and surrendering the treat. You can increase the count as you practice the sit-stay and the stand-stay commands in the weeks to come.

Sniffing and possibly mouthing each other are normal behaviors as pups meet and get to know each other.

A puppy training class will introduce your pup to new playmates in a controlled environment.

Sometimes pups will share a toy peacefully; other times they might play-fight over the toy to establish which is the dominant pup.

Meeting children is a necessary part of every puppy's socialization process. Well-behaved children who have been properly instructed on how to handle a puppy are the only young people to whom your puppy should be introduced.

shoulders. Children need to be told not to pet the dog on top of the head in a threatening manner or around his mouth, which will encourage him to chew on their little fingers. Remind the children not to pick up the puppy unless they're given permission to do so, and then show them how to handle a puppy correctly by supporting the hindquarters with one hand.

Keep your voice happy and a smile on your face as you go about the neighborhood. Your puppy will read this cheeriness toward other people as a signal that all is well and that greeting people is an enjoyable experience. Be sure to praise your puppy when he wags his tail and exhibits friendliness.

The shy puppy needs some special handling to overcome his lack of self-confidence. Take a pocketful of treats with you when you go out. When you meet someone, give the person a treat and ask him to offer the biscuit to your puppy. If the puppy is too stressed when he begins socializing, he won't be able to swallow a treat. But, with your encouragement, he'll soon accept the neighbor's treat (that you provided) and look forward to visiting people who he meets.

Never pick up the puppy or coddle him when he displays shyness or timidity in this new situation. If you do, the puppy will read that behavior as "It's okay to be scared. The boss will pick me up every time I show him how scared I am." Soon, the puppy will figure out that all he has to do to get you to pick him up is to act scared. Simply ignore his timid behavior and act happily so that he begins to take on the same feeling of excitement that you show. Praising him when he does

this will cement the notion that being friendly and outgoing is the way to seek positive attention. (Remember the old axiom to ignore that which you don't want repeated?)

Once the puppy feels comfortable with socializing in the neighborhood, take him to a shopping center. There, you'll meet lots of people and, since most of them love puppies, it will be easy to

A nine-week-old Basenji puppy is fairly reserved and shy compared to puppies of many other breeds. Such a puppy will require more careful supervision during socialization encounters.

encourage them to pet your dog and talk to him. Be sure to take some of his treats along and have the new people you meet offer the puppy a treat when he accepts their attention.

FEEDING METHODS

There are two ways to feed a dog, either the scheduled method or the free-feed method. Whether you're feeding a puppy or an adult dog, it's helpful to know the pros and cons of both.

Free-feeding means simply pouring some dry kibble in a bowl whenever the contents of the bowl get low. You do not have to watch the dog eat or pay attention to when the dog eats. He's free to eat whenever he is hungry. There are some dogs, however, that cannot handle the free-feed method because they will eat until they almost explode. They get sick from overeating and then lose all the nutrition they ingested in the first place.

Scheduled feeding is much more structured. You prepare a certain amount of food, several times a day. You offer it to the dog and leave the bowl down for a specific amount of time, preferably 15 minutes, no more. At the end of that time, you remove the bowl and offer no more food until the next scheduled feeding time. If the dog fools around and

This young bloodhound seems to be quite fond of his young master. Some puppies are more demonstrative than others.

A NATURAL PROTECTOR

For one reason or another, some people don't want their puppy to befriend strangers, thinking that, when the puppy grows up, he won't be protective of home and family. This is not what happens. The puppy needs to know that all people are nice and friendly. When he's mature and he finds himself in a threatening situation, such as a  stranger breaking into his home, he will do whatever he must do to prevent the person from entering the home. He will not need to be taught to be protective if you build a strong bond with him when he's young and teach him that people are nice by acting friendly toward them. Develop a bond of friendship and trust with your puppy now, and he'll take whatever action is necessary later. Taking your puppy with you when you visit gas stations, newsstands, hardware stores, etc., will add to his repertoire of experiences.

does not finish his meal when it's served, he'll lose some of it when you remove the bowl. However, he'll only do that for a few days until he realizes that he'd better get right to eating when that bowl goes down. Most dogs learn to concentrate on eating the entire meal as soon as it's offered. They do not wander away or become distracted when the food bowl is presented.

Free-feeding does not allow you the opportunity to control the dog's diet, so you never really know how much he's eating or when. In addition, since he eats intermittently throughout the day and night, he has no schedule for bowel movements and that can make house-training very difficult.

Scheduled feeding allows you to know exactly how often the dog eats and the amount he consumes at each feeding. Since your feedings are served on a schedule, his elimination process becomes voluntarily scheduled as well. Consequently, house-training becomes so much easier. Finally, an important advantage to scheduled feeding is the fact that you can keep an eye on the dog's daily health. By observing the

Just as in everything you do with your puppy, consistency is important in his feeding schedule.

times when he refuses food, you can be warned of approaching ill health and act accordingly in advance of serious health problems.

MOUTHING

Mouthing and chewing are common puppy behaviors. Each has a different cause, and each behavior must be addressed separately. Mouthing occurs when puppies are teething and their gums ache. Mouthing on your hands, arms, clothes, etc., helps relieve some of their discomfort. If allowed to continue, mouthing can become a more serious problem that may end up in biting behavior as an adult. To stop the puppy

from mouthing, we take two types of approaches.

First, whenever your puppy mouths your hands or arms, yelp in a high-pitched voice. That's the sound his littermates would make if he were too rough with them. Turn away for a minute so that he knows that when he's too rough, play stops.

Petting the dog on the head and around the face will only encourage him to mouth your hand, so get in the habit of petting him just behind his neck, in the shoulder area. If he doesn't see your hand, he's less likely to want to chew on it. This whole matter will die out naturally around the puppy's 16th week of age, when he

THE "HOTDOG" TRICK

One little trick I use is to make frozen "hotdogs" for my puppies. They're easy to make and don't cost anything except a few minutes of my time.

Take several pieces of terry cloth that measure 7 or 8 inches square. Wet them thoroughly and then squeeze them out until they stop dripping but are still very wet. Lay them out on a counter and roll each one separately into a cigar-shaped cylinder. Place them in the freezer compartment of the refrigerator and freeze until they're solid.

Offer a frozen "hotdog" to the teething puppy whenever he seems to want to chew on something such as a toy or forbidden object. The coolness of the frozen roll will soothe his gums and the softness of the terry cloth will give him something chewable. As soon as the hotdog is thawed and floppy, replace it with another frozen one. Rewet the first one and return it to the refrigerator to freeze again.

begins to lose those puppy teeth and the adult ones emerge. Until that time, he feels very uncomfortable while the new teeth are developing and the baby teeth are getting ready to fall out.

The second approach to mouthing is diversion. When the puppy begins mouthing you or anyone else, get his mind off the behavior by asking him a question such as, "Where's your fluffy? Go get your fluffy" (or "bouncy" or whatever toy he really likes).

If this doesn't dissuade him from mouthing, get his mind on something new by taking him for a walk or playing a fetch game with him. Anything that will get his mind off mouthing and onto something positive will alter the situation and offer you an opportunity to interact with him in a positive manner.

CHEWING

Chewing on items that are not permissible, such as the arm of a chair or the leg of a table, must be stopped as soon as possible. Chewing on electrical cords, telephone, computer and TV wiring, and light plugs not only is dangerous but also can cause house fires, even death to the puppy.

Again, puppies chew because they're teething and their gums hurt. They prefer to chew on soft things like pillows, clothes, shoes, and upholstered furniture, but when available, they'll chew on anything they can get their mouths on!

How cute is this puppy chewing on his mistress's shoelace? Not cute at all! You must enforce the "no-chew" rule from the onset, or your dog will grow up thinking he can sharpen his canines on any object he wishes.

Another very common reason for chewing is the release of anxiety. Frustration is a serious problem in young dogs and can be managed in most cases by an understanding owner. The frustration of being left alone in the house while the owner is gone often manifests itself in the dog's chewing something to relieve his anxiety.

Owners frequently remark that when their puppy chews up forbidden items while he's alone, the puppy is being spiteful. First, dogs do not experience the emotion of spite. They simply express their anxieties in a physical activity such as chewing, eliminating, incessant barking, or digging up carpeting or furniture cushions.

When the owner returns and discovers that the puppy has wreaked havoc in the house, the owner becomes angry and disciplines the dog for such a naughty act. The fact that the dog did the damage hours ago means that the dog will not be able to associate the "damage" with the resulting discipline. Consequently, the dog relates the discipline to the owner's returning home. If this scenario occurs often enough, the dog will believe that the owner is going to punish or discipline him every time he comes home. Associating the punishment with the crime is lost on the dog, and he then begins to dislike and avoid his owner. Thus, punishing the puppy after the fact should never be done.

As grim as all these problems seem to be, there is a very simple and easy solution. What's more, puppy and owner will not experience the trauma of ineffective, harsh punishment that ultimately destroys the dog-owner relationship.

The answer? Crate-train your puppy starting with the first day you bring him home. He should be in his crate whenever you cannot be with him or be supervising his activities. The fact that he's in his own place of security prevents anxiety, which, in turn, prevents chewing and destruction caused by frustration. He will quickly learn to love his safe little cubby and settle down in it as soon as you put him there. Providing you've taken him out to relieve himself before you put him in his crate, he'll probably fall asleep as soon as you're gone. Since there's nothing to do and no one around to distract him, he'll use the quiet time to rest.

As soon as you return or become available to interact with him again, take him out of his crate and go directly outside to his relief area. Once he's relieved himself, he'll be ready to come indoors and be with you once more. Most people who live with crate-trained dogs say they wouldn't dream of living with a dog that wasn't crate-trained. Crates are ideal management tools in the home, and they serve a wonderful purpose away from the home. When you go on vacation with your dog, take his crate along and he'll be content to stay in his crate whenever you leave him, despite the fact that he's in an unfamiliar environment.

Although you should always supervise your pup with soft toys, as they can often be "de-stuffed" rather easily, soft toys are ideal for young puppies who are teething.

Remember, his crate (his personal environment) is always familiar to him! Crates make the world a safer, more secure place for all—dogs, owners, and their possessions!

THINGS TO DO

WEEK 2

- Practice exercises from the previous week.
- Teach "Sit-stay."
- Teach "Stand-stay."
- Begin socialization away from home.
- Introduce puppy to children, other pets.
- Evaluate your puppy's feeding method.
- Address mouthing and chewing behaviors.

Again, there's an exciting week ahead for you and your puppy. We'll work on some control lessons and introduce walking beside you without pulling. We'll find some new and intriguing footing that the puppy has never experienced. We'll also address the problem of puppy's jumping up on people to greet them and onto furniture that's off-limits.

TEACH "DOWN"

Before teaching the puppy to lie down on command, you need to know how dogs perceive the down position. In the wild, for example, a dog would only lie down when and where he felt completely secure. If there was some strange animal or person in the area, he would immediately be up on his feet because instinct would tell him that he may have to fight or flee for his own safety. The dog's being in a down position would give his adversary an advantage, so the dog would be on his feet, ready to respond to whatever circumstances might occur.

Therefore, in teaching the down, we provide a quiet, safe environment for the lesson. For that reason, we say "Down" very quietly and introduce the exercise in a neutral place inside the home. Choose a time when there's a minimum of activity going on around you so that the puppy doesn't feel threatened. Some dogs may see the down exercise as a form of submission and refuse to do it. A shy, timid puppy may fear the down exercise to the point of running from you when you attempt to have him lie down. The fearful puppy may attempt to bite you if you force him to lie down.

By using a motivational method of teaching the down, each puppy learns to obey willingly and enjoy the exercise because it represents praise and treats when it's completed. You will probably find it easier to teach the down exercise when the puppy is hungry rather than after a full meal. He'll want that food treat more before a meal, so he'll be anxious to drop down to get it.

One of the key components of training a dog is making sure his attention is focused solely on you.

▲ Begin the down command with the dog sitting, just as you would if teaching him on the floor.

Have the dog sit next to you at your left side. Hold the lead loosely in your left hand with several pieces of food in your right hand. Place your left hand (still holding the lead loosely) gently on top of the dog's shoulders where they meet above the spinal cord and just below his neck. Do not push down with your left hand; just let it rest on the puppy's shoulders. Place your food hand at the puppy's nose and say, "Down," in a soft whisper. Slowly lower your food hand from the dog's nose to between his two front feet on the floor. Then, as the dog's nose follows the treat downward, slowly move your food hand out in front of the dog along the floor. As your hand moves forward, he'll reach further forward to get the treat.

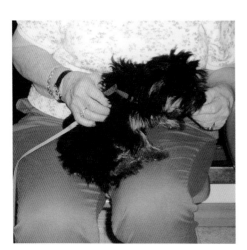

▲ Whether taught on your lap or on the floor, the pup will follow the treat forward until he naturally assumes the down position.

▲ Release the treat once the dog's elbows touch the floor—and don't forget to praise at the same time.

THE TOY FACTOR: DOWN

Even if you have a toy-breed puppy who absolutely refuses to lie down on the floor, we can use an alternative method to teach them down. It begins with the puppy's sitting on your lap and includes praise each step of the way. Hold the treat at the puppy's nose and slowly lower your hand down to a position below the level of your lap beside your thigh. The pup will follow the food hand and lower his front legs in order to reach the treat. Once he will drop in your lap, switch to have him lie down on the sofa beside you. Praise again.

With some puppies, when their front legs go down, their rear legs pop up. Try training at the top of a flight of stairs. Sit on a lower step and lure your puppy down by bringing your hand below their head level. Once they've mastered the down, you can work on the length of time they stay down.

At this point, he'll lower his front legs down to the floor in order to reach even further forward to get the treat. When his elbows touch the floor, release one piece of food and let him nibble the other pieces. As he nibbles, use your left hand to stroke him along his back and tell him what a good dog he is. Praise softly and stroke gently. We want the puppy to get used to doing the down and settling there rather than jumping up the minute he receives a treat. The down exercise is the exercise that will give you the most control.

HEELING

Heeling means that the dog walks beside you, usually on your left side, without pulling on the lead. As the dog matures and becomes good at heeling, he will eventually walk beside you without a lead. But for now and for the next several months, be sure to keep his lead on when heeling.

Because your puppy is so young, it would be very dangerous to use any kind of choke collar or forceful method to teach heeling. When the puppy pulls out ahead of you and the collar presses against his throat, it could cause permanent damage to his throat and neck. For this reason, we will use food to lure the puppy into the proper heeling position and to maintain it for short distances. Again, work with a hungry puppy for maximum success.

When a dog is attached to a lead and begins to pull out ahead of his owner, who

▲ These puppies are learning to heel, and they follow the treats as they walk along. The owners must hold the treat in the correct position so the pups stay by the owners' sides.

is holding the other end of the lead, the owner's reaction to the dog's pulling is to pull back. In fact, pulling back against the dog teaches him to pull more. When a dog pulls on his lead and feels his owner pulling back, the dog thinks he's supposed to pull even harder. Soon we have a situation in which the dog thinks he's got to pull his owner down the street as if the owner were a sled and he were a budding husky! For this reason, I never recommend walking a puppy on a retractable lead until he's learned how to heel beside his owner and not pull.

Teaching heeling correctly means that you will demonstrate to the puppy by your actions that you will not proceed forward unless the puppy is beside you. Having a treat in your left hand at the dog's nose will convince him that the heel position is the place to be.

To begin, hold the lead in your right hand and some treats in your left hand. Have the dog sit beside you on your left side and place the food hand at the dog's nose. First, say "Heel" or "Let's go" to the puppy and step out on your left foot. As you move forward, the puppy will get up and follow that food hand in front of his nose.

Take four or five steps and then stop. As you do, say, "Sit," to the puppy and raise your food hand up slightly over his head. As the puppy sits beside you, praise and give him a treat. Try not to pet him

A small-breed pup requires an owner to bend down further to keep the treat at the pup's nose.

during these stops. Instead, release the food and verbally praise in a soft voice. You don't want him to get up from the sit position, so keeping your voice low will not overly excite him and make him jump up. Hesitate for a few seconds and begin walking again. With your food hand at the puppy's nose, say "Heel" and step out as before. After a short distance, stop and have the puppy sit beside you once more, then give him praise and the treat immediately.

Repeat this process of starting, walking short distances, and stopping with the dog in the sit position beside you whenever he's not moving. We call the sitting position the heel position and, from now on, you'll recognize that all of the dog's exercises begin and end with his sitting at heel position. In other words, the heel position becomes home base to the dog for the rest of his life.

If, at any time, the puppy bolts forward and begins pulling, stop dead in your tracks and refuse to move. What you're saying here is that you will not go forward until the dog is beside you. Sooner or later, he'll get the idea and settle down to stay beside you. When you finish your heeling practice, release the dog from the heel position by praising him and saying "Okay, good boy!" Soon, he'll learn that "Okay" is a release-from-duty word and that he's free to relax when he hears it. When practicing the heel, don't overdo it. Spend a few minutes on heeling and then move on to something else before the puppy gets bored with it.

With an extremely stubborn dog that insists on pulling, it may take you quite a while to convince him that you are the leader and you will decide how fast you two will walk, and in which direction. I once had a student with a medium-sized dog that refused to stop pulling. She became as stubborn as the dog and spent three weeks taking one step and then stopping until the dog turned around and looked at her. At that point, she'd tell him, "Good boy," and take another step or two. During week four of this standoff, the dog looked at her one day and came to stand beside her as if to say, "You win." From that time on, he heeled beautifully beside her and only needed an occasional reminder not to pull.

Be patient with this lesson. Realize that it's going to take some time, but it's far safer and more pleasant for you both to act out the heeling process than to force the puppy into doing it. Teaching the puppy to walk politely without pulling while he's young is a lot more successful than when

Keeping the pup's attention is tantamount to executing a new lesson. "Watch me" is a vital lesson in the pup's continuing education.

he's mature and has been pulling you down the street for months. As you begin to increase the number of steps you two can take without his pulling on the lead, watch for signs that the puppy is beginning to comprehend the exercise. If he walks with you and there's a slack lead between you, tell him, "Good boy. Good heel." When he looks up at you, smile and say "Good."

TEACH "WATCH ME"

Paying attention to you and what you're doing is the first step in the pup's learning to work with you. His watching you as you walk together is a sure sign that he understands this partner relationship that you're building. One day, he'll rush to your side, tail wagging, when he hears the heel command. With or without his lead, he'll be there at your side as you stroll along together.

Reinforcing and expanding this "Watch me" lesson is easy. Have a food treat in your right hand so the puppy sees the food and the hand is lined up between his eyes and yours. When he looks at the food treat, he'll automatically see your face in the background. Repeat "Watch, watch me" several times so that he begins to associate the word "watch" with looking into your face. Shortly, he'll look at you whenever you tell him to "watch." When he does look at you, he can't be distracted by other things in his

Jumping up helps a dog get closer to the ones he loves! Discourage this behavior by having him sit, and then bending down to his level to let him be near you.

surroundings that would surely take his mind off you and what he's supposed to be doing. In short, he's focusing.

DISCOURAGING JUMPING UP

On People

Puppies jump up on people because they want to see them, be with them or get attention from them. It's a natural thing to do when you want someone to react to you. Early interactions with you quickly taught the puppy how to get your attention. Now you must teach the puppy that he'll get as much attention as he wants, but he must not jump up

THE JUNK-TRAP METHOD

The junk-trap method of teaching a puppy not to jump onto furniture is useful for the very stubborn fellow. This method takes a bit of setting up on your part, but it's fun to watch the puppy try to figure out the predicament he's gotten himself into when he jumps up on the sofa. Put the puppy in his crate so he can't see you set up the trap. Take pots and pans, pot lids, canned goods, large serving spoons (no forks or knives) and anything else that is safe, of an odd shape and/or noisy when it moves. Spread these items out across the sofa until the entire surface is covered with this collection of hard, oddly shaped objects.

Setting boundaries with your puppy will lead to lifelong good habits and fun times for both of you.

Now release the puppy from his crate and say nothing to him. Watch him from a distance and when he jumps up on the sofa because he thinks it's safe now that you're out of the room, he'll be faced with a collection of junk that is so diverse and uncomfortable that he'll be unable to find a place to settle down. Wherever he turns, he'll meet with hard metal items, things that rattle and shake. Nowhere will there be a soft cushiony place to rest. Shortly, he'll decide that the floor is a lot more comfortable than your sofa and he'll jump off the sofa. As soon as he does—remember, you're watching from a distance—go into the room and tell him what a good boy he is to be on the floor! Leave the junk-trap set up for a few days and the puppy will soon decide that the floor and his soft bed are more to his liking than your furniture.

Rewarding your pup for successfully following commands is essential to establishing lifelong good behavior.

on you or others. It's unpleasant to have a dog who jumps on people who come to visit. Jumping up on elderly people and children can cause them to fall and be hurt. Jumping on people after being outdoors in the rain will get people wet and muddy. Clearly not good things!

To teach your dog not to jump up on you, firmly order him to sit whenever he attempts to jump up. As soon as he does, praise him and give him a treat. If he jumps up without sitting, turn and walk away from him. Then turn back, repeat the command and give him his treat only when all four of his feet are on the ground. He'll soon figure out that sitting instead of jumping up on you produces a reward.

Remember, too, that jumping on you is the pup's way of saying that he wants to greet you and be close to you. Bending over and petting him is another way to satisfy his need for attention. Just be sure he sits before he receives your attention.

To teach your dog not to jump up on other people, have him on lead and arrange for a friend or neighbor to stop by. When the doorbell rings, attach the dog's lead, take a biscuit in your hand, and proceed to the door. Firmly command the dog to sit and reinforce the sit by using the lead to control him and keep him sitting. Allow your friend to enter and immediately give the person the biscuit. Once the dog is sitting (you may be physically holding him in that position the first few times), ask your friend to give the dog the biscuit and to say, "Good boy."

Soon, the dog will learn that when the doorbell rings, a nice person is coming to bring him a treat. He'll run to the door and sit automatically while waiting for you to admit the guest. You won't need to use the dog's lead for very long before he gets the idea that visitors come to see him (a puppy doesn't realize that people come to see you, too).

On the Furniture...Or Off?

Whether or not your dog is allowed on the furniture is up to you. Just remember that it is easier to teach something than it is to break a habit. If you won't want your adult dog on the furniture, don't let your puppy on it. Don't scoop him up for a cuddle on the couch. Don't lift him up when wants to join you in the chair. If you see him getting ready to jump up, call him, ask him to do something else, and reward him for that.

If you don't mind some dog hair on the upholstery, and want your dog beside you in the evening, that's fine. You don't need to train him to join you; he'll want to. In consideration of guests, you might want to cover the sofa or chair where your dog

There's nothing wrong with wanting your cuddly friend to sit beside you on the couch. But remember that it's easier to teach expectations when the dog is a puppy than it is to correct a bad habit when they're an adult.

routinely curls up with an easy-to-wash throw or with towels.

The same goes for your bed. If you don't want your dog on the bed, don't let your puppy there. If you'd enjoy sleeping with your dog, cover your bedspread with a sheet, or something else that's easy to wash and invite him up. Dogs are individuals and maybe your dog won't want to share your bed anyway. Either way, the choice is yours.

WALKS OF LIFE

Helping your puppy to build his self-confidence is an important step in developing your dog to his fullest potential. Teaching him to cope with strange footing is one more way of showing him that he can face whatever life presents.

Find a variety of places with different kinds of terrain and allow your puppy to investigate them and walk on the different surfaces. Such surfaces as cement, stone, grass, boardwalks, sand, stone paths, and even sheets of slippery black plastic will serve as training experiences. You can take a large black plastic bag, cut it open, and lay it out on the floor. Put the puppy on lead and, with you at his side, approach the plastic. Encourage him to smell it and feel it until he's no longer hesitant about approaching it. Then walk across the plastic together and praise him as you go. The first time he does it, he'll be reluctant, but he'll probably go with you if your voice is calm, confident and casual. "Oh, look, this is plastic. Let's walk on it." The second time he walks across the plastic, he may even stop and try to grab at it to play when he sees that it is harmless.

The bottom line here is that the more he experiences during puppyhood, the more confident he'll be as an adult. Each time he has a new experience, he gets closer to becoming a dog that's sure of himself and the world he lives in.

THINGS TO DO

WEEK 3

- Practice all previous exercises.
- Teach "Down."
- Teach heeling.
- Teach "Watch me."
- Practice no jumping on people and furniture.
- Introduce strange-footing experiences.

Puppy Training
The Fourth Week

Take the down and add a stay to it, and you have this week's lesson. By now, the puppy is familiar with the sit-stay and stand-stay, so the down-stay is an easy lesson for most puppies. "Agility" is the new word this week. The puppy will have some fun experiences ahead of him as well as a new trick he can learn. Remember that the more the puppy learns, the more easily he will be able to learn new things until learning itself becomes a breeze and he's always eager to try new experiences. A new way to approach feeding time and meeting your neighbor will finish out the lessons this week.

TEACH "DOWN-STAY"

Once again, food and praise will be used to show the puppy exactly what is expected in the down-stay. Corrections are counterproductive to learning, so help the puppy learn his lessons correctly and celebrate each small step until he reaches the goal of each lesson.

Begin with the puppy sitting on your left side as described for the down exercise. Have several pieces of food in your right

hand and guide the puppy into the down position. As soon as the puppy goes down, keep your food hand in front of his nose, release one piece of food and say "Stay." Step out on your right foot to pivot in front of the dog. Keep that food hand motionless in front of his nose—if you move it so much as an inch, he'll get up to follow the food and break his down. Count to five while you're in front of him, then return to stand beside him at heel position. While he's still lying down, release the food reward and praise as always.

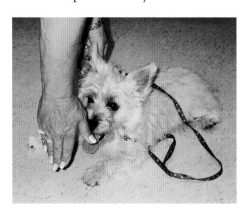

Along with your verbal command, the food hand at the dog's nose acts as a stay signal as you step out in front of the dog.

Agility training utilizes your pup's natural instincts to instill confidence in your dog, all while having fun!

This exercise takes place indoors. Take kitchen chairs and place them so their backs face each other about 12 inches apart. Take an old bed sheet or blanket and drape it over the two chairs so that it falls down to the floor on both sides. This will create a tunnel. You can also use a

card table or a rectangular table if you have one. Draping a sheet over the top of it so the sheet falls to the floor on either side will create the tunnel.

Have someone hold the puppy on lead at one end of the tunnel while you go to the other end. Bend down so the puppy sees your face at the other end when he looks into the tunnel. With a couple of treats in your hand, coax the puppy to come through the tunnel to you at the opposite end to receive his reward. Incidentally, kids love to crawl in and out of the tunnel with the puppy, too!

At first, the puppy may be hesitant to enter the obstacle. To the puppy, the tunnel looks like a big mouth that will swallow him up as he enters! He probably thinks that the sides of it will close in around him if he goes inside. If he's reluctant to enter, reach inside and get the treat close to his mouth. When he reaches for it, slowly bring your food hand back out and he'll follow it. Once through, praise lavishly and enthusiastically celebrate his bravery. The next time, he won't hesitate at all. In fact, he may soon get to the point where he will run ahead of you through the tunnel when he sees that you've set it up for him. For variety, try setting up the tunnel in different places in the house and then in your yard.

AGILITY

Agility is an activity used for fun and to build the dog's self-confidence. Learning that he can negotiate various obstacles demonstrates to the dog that he can cope with whatever obstacles life presents. Soon, the puppy becomes immune to the height, depth, or length of an obstacle. He just knows that he loves running through the obstacle course and that he can't wait for a turn to show you how good he is at agility. In agility, you, the owner, will run alongside the puppy as he takes on the various obstacles. Your job will be to give commands and guide the puppy from one obstacle to another as you run through the course.

If you really enjoy agility, you can join a competitive agility team and race against other teams in timed trials. Kennel clubs in many countries offer titles to dogs who excel in agility. However, if you choose never to compete in agility with your dog, both of you will still derive great pleasure and lots of good, healthy exercise from individual agility obstacles.

Before pursuing agility trials as a competitive sport, it is important to realize that a dog must be 12 months of age before he can participate. Also, as bone development is different for each breed, ask your vet at what age it is safe to begin agility training with your particular pup to avoid stress and potential harm to his growing limbs.

Because your dog is a young puppy, we will keep things simple and be sure not to overwork the dog. He can learn to develop speed and jumping skills once he's a mature adult, but for now we just want him to have fun and become confident.

(Top) A plastic barrel, the top and bottom of which have been removed, makes a great introductory tunnel. (Bottom) As your pup becomes comfortable, you can use a longer tunnel. These types are often collapsible and easy to transport. Always let your puppy see the treat at the end of the tunnel!

MEET YOUR NEIGHBOR

When you're walking your dog outdoors and you come upon a person, who may or may not be accompanied by a dog, teach your dog to sit quietly beside you while you greet the other person. When the person sees you teaching your dog good manners, he may teach his own dog the same behavior. That way, you two can chat freely as your dogs lie or sit quietly beside you without interfering with each other or the other person.

To begin this lesson, go outside and arrange for a family member or friend to meet you as you walk along with the puppy. When you reach each other, have the dog sit or lie down beside you. Make small talk for a brief period, and then praise and treat your puppy for his patience and good behavior.

As soon as the puppy becomes accustomed to this type of greeting behavior when he's outdoors with you, change the training scenario so that you meet people who are unfamiliar to the puppy. He must learn to display good manners in the presence of strangers as well as those people he knows. That way,

A polite puppy will sit or lie down patiently while his master meets up with a friend or stranger. This type of mannerly behavior must be practiced.

TEACH "GIVE ME YOUR PAW"

Here's an easy trick to teach your dog that will be entertaining for your guests and have a practical application throughout the dog's life. Nail trimming is an essential part of canine maintenance. Teaching the dog to allow you to hold his paw while you trim his toenails will be a lot less stressful than forcibly holding the dog's foot for the procedure.

Begin with the dog sitting in front of you. Hold a treat in your left hand so he can see it. Reach your right hand down to the dog's foot and slide your fingers behind the paw. When he feels you touch his foot, he'll pick it up. At that point, keep your right hand open with the dog's paw resting in your hand. Do not try to hold the foot, as this will make him resist and pull his foot away from your hand. Keep your hand beneath his paw momentarily and then give him the treat with lots of praise. Repeat several times, and the dog will make the association that your words "Give me your paw" mean that he should place his foot in your hand.

Only after the dog is well adjusted to giving you either paw and holding it in your palm for several seconds should you attempt nail trimming. Always trim the nails a little at a time to avoid cutting into the quick and causing the nail to bleed. Your veterinarian or a professional groomer can show you how to trim nails

When your puppy meets another dog or puppy, supervise the encounter but do not interfere. Canine meeting rituals are thousands of years old, and do not require your pulling on the lead or yanking at the dogs. Dog fights are usually inadvertently instigated by overly concerned owners.

he will always be welcome to accompany you wherever you go once he's a mature adult.

You may one day decide that you'd like to get involved in dog therapy work. You and your dog volunteer to visit people in hospitals, homes, schools and the like. Having a well-mannered dog who can accept almost any type of situation and act politely around all people, familiar or not, will be the key to successful therapy work.

Teaching your dog to give his paw upon command is a simple and fun exercise, with practical benefits as well.

before you try it yourself. As you trim each nail, reward the dog's cooperation with a treat. With a nervous-type puppy, it will be better to trim only one foot each day so he doesn't become too stressed over the procedure. Learning to trust you in all areas of life is important in the puppy's development.

TEACH "SIT-STAY" AT FEEDING TIME

I'm sure you realize by now that a behavior we teach the puppy one week may well become part of a more sophisticated exercise in another week. Therefore, it's important to practice all exercises every week. Each time you do, you help the puppy transfer the things he learns from his short-term memory to his long-term (for life) memory. Such is the case with this exercise.

So far, you've taught the puppy to do a simple sit-stay with you standing in front of him. Now we'll extend that behavior to include a sit-stay while you prepare his meals.

At mealtime, allow the puppy to come into the kitchen with you. Give him a sit-stay near where you're working and proceed with the food preparation. If he will not stay in the sit position and wait to be served, you'll need some help to get the lesson's message across. Put the puppy on collar and lead and have a family member hold the dog in a sit-stay while you prepare his meal. If you don't have someone to help you, tie the puppy to a door or other object. He probably won't sit, but he'll surely stay. Once he gets the idea that you will not release him until you're ready, he'll settle down and sit without an order from you. When you do release him, praise him for sitting and waiting.

Soon you won't need to restrain the puppy. He'll learn that sitting and staying is the quickest way to get his dinner. When you release him, use the word "Okay" as a signal to end the stay.

If you have trained your puppy properly, he can pass the supreme test of sit-stay on his way to his food bowl.

This Okay command should always be used whenever you release him from any command.

THINGS TO DO

WEEK 4

- Practice all previous exercises.
- Teach "Down-stay."
- Introduce agility with the tunnel.
- Introduce meeting your neighbors.
- Teach "Give me your paw" and introduce nail trimming.
- Teach "Sit-stay" at feeding time.

Puppy Training
The Fifth Week

PLAY "PASS THE PUPPY"

This game is a great way to get your puppy used to coming when called, and it teaches him that, when people call him, he will get a treat. Gather up friends and neighbors and have everyone sit on the floor in a circle with the puppy in the middle. Make sure each person has a good supply of tiny treats. Call your puppy to you, using an excited voice. When he comes, give him some love and a treat. Then, someone across the circle calls your puppy, following the same pattern. Your puppy gets used to lots of people and learns that good things happen when he is called and obeys.

You can also play a variation of this game with just household members. Wait until your puppy is in another room and call him excitedly. Then, have another family member call the puppy, maybe even upstairs, depending on whether your puppy can easily manage stairs. You want the game to be super fun and easy for your puppy to play. When he does come, add the "gotcha" move of holding his collar for just a moment.

While most of the time you should only use one command to a dog, during these games, keep up a happy stream of chatter. If you're playing between rooms, this will help the puppy find the person calling him. We are not in a serious training mode; we want the puppy to have fun and to succeed in reaching the person calling. As your puppy gets used to this game, people can hide behind furniture or in closets (with the door open). Make up your own variations of this game. Your puppy will love it, and he'll be learning to come when called.

As your dog matures, you can change the game to one of "find" and ask your dog to "find Timmy." With only a little encouragement, he'll search for and find individual family members. Remember, NEVER call your dog for something he finds unpleasant. If you need to cut his nails, and he hates that, go and get him.

By the time your puppy becomes an adolescent (five to eight months of age), he'll be ready to play the game outdoors. Be sure to play it in an enclosed area, such

With training, your pup can learn to find toys, treats, and even family members!

"Where are you?" is a game that never fails when you want your dog to come to you. This method is much less stressful than simply teaching your puppy to come on command.

as a fenced yard. Never trust the outdoor environment as being completely safe for your dog. You never know when an unfriendly dog will appear out of nowhere, or a strange cat will come strolling out from behind a bush. In any case, these things can spell trouble for you and your dog, so be sure to have an enclosed area where you have control and where the pup can't run off after something that catches his interest.

WAITING AT DOORWAYS, STAIRS AND CARS

While we're on the subject of keeping your puppy safe, let's take this idea a step further and exercise your leader role in a new direction. Reinforcing the concept that you make life decisions for your puppy should be demonstrated frequently to your dog in subtle ways. Each time you and your puppy enter a car, walk through a doorway, or go up or down a stairway together, the dog should wait until you tell him it's okay to follow you. Not only does this keep your puppy safe from harm, it prevents the puppy from causing human accidents when he nudges you out of the way so he can go first. You can imagine what would happen if a large dog were to push an elderly lady out of his way as they passed through a doorway. The lady could fall and be seriously hurt.

WAIT AT A DOORWAY

To teach the dog to wait until he's told to proceed, have him on his collar and lead. Initially you can use food treats, but this should not be required for long. Remember that he's already been taught to stay, and the "wait" is a close relative. Approach a closed door with your dog on lead. Tell him to sit and show him the open palm of your right hand as you say, "Stay. Wait." Step away from your dog and open the door as you remind him to "Stay. Wait." Keep that stay-signal hand in front of him to reinforce the stay-wait. Now open the door and step through the doorway. Keep reminding him to wait. He may want to break the stay at this point because he thinks you're about to leave him. Just be firm with your command and insist that he stay seated where he is, even if you have to correct him several times.

Once you're through the doorway, say, "Okay, good boy." At that point, he'll eagerly join you on the other side of the doorway. Give him a treat and praise generously when he gets beside you. It should only take the puppy a few days to learn this lesson, providing you give your stay-wait command firmly and praise lavishly when he succeeds.

A properly trained puppy will not go through a doorway without your permission to do so.

▲ A puppy's charging ahead without you is neither mannerly nor safe behavior.

▲ A puppy's proper place while walking is at his owner's side unless he is told to "wait."

Wait at a Stairway

Once the dog masters sitting and waiting at doorways, he's ready to sit and wait at stairways. The idea here is for the dog to wait until you go either up or down the stairs before he's permitted to join you. Shoving you out of the way on a stairway can cause a bad fall. Teach him to wait by rewarding and praising his success at each small step of the learning process.

During the stairway training, put the puppy on a long line. The line must be long enough to control him over the entire length of the stairway. Most pet-supply stores sell long lines in lengths of 25, 35, and 50 feet. You can make your own long line, too. Purchase a length of nylon cording from a hardware store. Tie a loop at one end of the cord and a metal clasp at the other end. (The clasp can probably be purchased at the same store.) Begin either at the top or bottom of the stairs and have your dog sit. Tell him to "Stay. Wait." and go down two steps as your stay-signal hand reminds him with your voice to "wait." When he'll stay seated while you go down two steps, try going down four steps. Gradually increase the number of steps away from the dog you can take until you're all the way down the stairs.

Once he's successful at waiting while you go down the stairs, reverse the training and teach him to wait while you go up the stairs. Most puppies do better at waiting at the top of a stairway than waiting at the bottom. However, they can and do learn to wait in both directions and you should pursue this goal until he understands that you always proceed him at stairways. Again be generous with your praise for each lesson learned.

Wait at a Car

Teaching your puppy to wait while getting in and out of a car is an important lesson. Begin as before with the puppy on lead. Have him wait while you open the door

Part of training to wait includes the dog's not entering or exiting a car until his owner tells him to do so. This is so important, as your dog's safety relies upon his obeying this command.

The pup sits patiently by the open car door, looking up at his owner and awaiting her word that it is okay to get in.

and then tell him to "Hup" or "Load up." When you arrive at your destination, have the puppy wait again while you exit the car and then direct him to come out after you. A treat and praise when he obeys will help him master this exercise quickly because he's become accustomed to waiting at doorways and stairways prior to this lesson.

A NEW EXPERIENCE

Another new experience for your puppy is on the agenda for this week. It should be something that your puppy has never done before—a new taste, a new sound, a new place, a new activity, a new person coming into his life, etc. These new opportunities are what make up the backbone of your dog's ability to face and cope with so many different experiences in life. Each new experience should be introduced as something that's interesting and fun. Each new thing should evoke the dog's curiosity and willingness to investigate and ultimately accept them as part of life.

The precise experience you'll give your puppy this week will be decided by you. Try to find things, places, and people that interest you and base your lesson on one of them. Here are some ideas: Take your puppy to a ice cream shop for a lick of vanilla ice cream (never give your puppy chocolate, as it contains a chemical that

Taking your puppy out to new places helps him gain confidence in experiencing the unknown and find joy in adventure.

Dogs on the catwalk! Although not as nimble as their feline counterparts, dogs can be trained to handle this obstacle with encouragement, practice, and lots of praise and treats.

is poisonous to dogs and can be lethal). Arrange to meet a friend and his dog in a park—just be sure the other dog is friendly. Take your puppy out on a boat ride or to the beach. Whatever you decide to do, make sure the result is fun and positive for your puppy. If he acts hesitantly at any time, don't coddle him. Just assure him that all is well and proceed with the plan with a happy, confident tone of voice.

TEACH A NEW GAME

Here's a new game that will prove fun, rewarding, and challenging to your puppy. The goal of this "Find the toy" game is to have the puppy locate by scent one of his favorite toys which is completely hidden from sight, yet easily found if he uses his scenting ability (his nose).

Eventually, you can broaden this game and have the puppy locate and retrieve items belonging to you or other family members. Imagine how proud he'll be when he finds your "lost" glasses case or

The seesaw or teeter-totter (top two photos) and an A-frame (bottom photo) are standard obstacles in agility trials. Introducing your pup to either of these can be a fun new experience. (Don't forget your bag of treats!)

notebook! And it all begins now with a simple game of finding a partially hidden toy. Be sure your puppy is not in the room when you hide his toy. Place the toy somewhere in the room, but it should be hidden from his view. For instance, partially hide his favorite toy under the cushion of a chair with part of it sticking out beyond the edge of the seat.

Tell the puppy to "Find fluffy" (or whatever name you've given the toy).

With the puppy on lead, walk him past the chair and, using your hand to get his attention onto the chair, encourage him to look at the chair's edge and see "fluffy" sticking out from under the cushion. When he sniffs it, encourage him to pull it out from its hiding place and carry it away in his mouth.

Lots of verbal praise and a treat will reinforce his achievement. Repeat the game, but, each time hide the toy in a

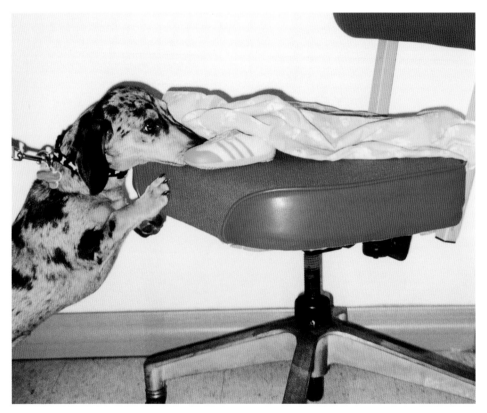

Finding the toy is a fun game for every puppy, and most excel right away, especially those blessed with a keen nose like this pup.

GOOD VIBRATIONS

Your attitude and acceptance toward teaching your puppy will greatly influence the puppy's final success. You have to be enthusiastic about training and introducing new positive experiences. Behaviorists and psychologists have determined that 60–80% of who you are and what you are feeling travels down the lead to your dog. No wonder dog people say, "You can fool people, but you can't fool your dog!"

different place and always partially hidden. Play this game for several days and always make sure the puppy wins by finding the toy. Losing the game will discourage him and he'll quit trying, but winning will urge him to even bigger challenges. Increase the difficulty so that eventually the toy is completely out of sight and the puppy is using his nose to find it. As he perfects his scenting skills and you witness his scenting ability, you'll find the game as much fun as the dog does.

THINGS TO DO

WEEK

5

- Practice all previous exercises.
- Teach the "Where are you?" game.
- Teach waiting at doorways, stairways and cars.
- Introduce a new experience.
- Teach a new game—scenting.

Puppy Training
The Sixth Week

TREAT WEANING

This is the week we begin to wean the puppy off the regular use of food treats in training. Food is always used to teach new behaviors, so in this case, we will wean off food in the behaviors he's been doing for a number of weeks, not new exercises. We will use a method that will gradually reduce the number of times and amounts of food treats that the puppy receives during the execution of familiar exercises. Most importantly, the verbal praise and physical petting you give for approval will always be necessary. The use of treats will gradually lessen until you no longer need food in your daily interactions with him. However, your voice will always reward his good behavior.

Variable-Ratio Reward System

Just as the name implies, food will now be used on a variable schedule so that the puppy never knows when he'll receive a treat for performing an exercise. This method is the same one used with people who play slot-machine games. They keep putting money into the machine in the hopes that it will pay off with a big reward. The eternal hope that the next time will be the one that produces a big win is the same principle for man as it is for dogs.

Further, as we decrease the use of food when the dog is told to do a certain behavior, the behavior itself becomes more and more a regular part of his lifestyle. Eventually, we won't think of the behaviors as exercises—they'll just be part of his normal, everyday life.

Begin by having the dog do a sit-stay. Instead of holding a food treat in front of the dog's nose, use your right hand with an open palm facing the dog and say, "Stay." That open palm will be the stay signal for the dog forever. If you remember, it's the same hand that held the food treat during those first five weeks of training. Now, the hand remains the same, but the food is gone and the palm is open.

Count to 10 and go back to the dog. Tell him, "Good boy! Good stay!" Pet and praise him excitedly. Finally, say, "Let's go get a biscuit," at which point you step

With enough training, your pup will learn to obey commands without needing the reward of a treat.

A telling test of your dog's training: obeying without food! Here's an obedience sit-stay (without a treat).

over to a nearby table and retrieve a biscuit for him. What you're doing here is still giving him the treat, but you're not holding it in your hand and it takes a few extra seconds to go get the treat for him. The subtle delaying of the food reward is the beginning of getting the puppy accustomed to receiving verbal praise and petting without food.

Repeat the sit-stay exercise just as before, but this time do not offer a treat after the conclusion. Lots of verbal praise and petting now substitute for the treat.

Do the sit-stay a third time and, when you return to the puppy, praise and pet him generously. When you've finished praising him, once again take him to a nearby table or chair and give him a biscuit as you say, "Let's get a biscuit." What we're doing here is alternating the times when we give food treats so that the puppy never knows when he'll receive a treat for any given exercise. By this method, he'll learn that he never knows when a treat will be forthcoming, so it's always best to obey the boss's commands.

In weaning the puppy off the food for any exercise, vary the times when you reward him with food so that he never knows when he'll receive a treat. Introduce the variable-ratio reward system in the sit-stay, the down-stay and the stand-stay exercises. These are all exercises he learned many weeks ago and

Obeying his master's hand signal to stand-stay (with no scent of liver within nose-shot).

he should be totally familiar with them by now. Do not vary the food when teaching a new exercise, as food reinforces the dog's obedience with a new behavior. As new exercises become more familiar and easy for him, you can apply the variable-ratio system to them until, finally, he no longer needs food for any of the exercises learned in the puppy program. However, throughout his life, he'll respond best to new work if you start by using food in his training.

NEUTERING AND SPAYING

Did you know there are more dogs turned over to animal shelters for behavior problems than for any other reason? A major portion of those behavior problems is caused by the dogs' being sexually intact rather than spayed or neutered. When you allow a dog to mature with his hormonal development intact, he or she often becomes unmanageable at maturity.

Females normally come into estrus twice a year, and each cycle lasts for approximately three weeks. During that time, they attract any and all males, who will camp outside your home and urinate all over the shrubbery and flowers. Fights among them are common, and their constant howling puts the whole neighborhood on edge.

A young puppy only has eyes for his owner, but your puppy's interest in you (and your lesson plans) will diminish as his hormones take over his brain. Discuss neutering or spaying your pet with your vet.

CONSULT YOUR VET

One additional and very important aspect of neutering and spaying is the health aspect to the dogs. Ovarian and testicular cancer do not occur in altered dogs, and the risk of breast and prostate cancer dramatically decreases. This factor, in itself, is reason enough to protect your puppy from future suffering.

Some humane societies are neutering and spaying puppies as young as 12 weeks old, some even as early as 8 weeks old. Most vets will often choose to do it when the puppy is 5 or 6 months of age. Check with your vet to find out at what age he will neuter or spay your puppy. With some large-breed dogs, spaying or neutering should wait until they are at least one year old. Spaying too early can affect growth plates, especially in the legs.

The veterinary charge is not expensive and is worth every penny you spend for it. The operation is more involved for bitches than dogs, though both procedures are considered routine.

In order to locate females in season, males will wander, sometimes for miles, following the scent of the females. Once bred by one of these roaming males, the female then produces a litter of unwanted puppies, which often end up in an animal shelter and eventually are euthanized because there just aren't enough people to adopt all of the puppies born by accident.

The solution, of course, is very simple. Males should be neutered and females spayed as soon as the veterinarian says it's time. Following the procedure, many good things happen both for the dog and for the owner. Males do not develop the habit and desire to wander. They are content to stay close to home and focus on their human pack. In addition, males are more manageable and easier to live with. Interestingly, they remain just as dedicated to protecting their homes and families as intact males. Neutered males are just easier to control. Spayed females do not come into season, thereby avoiding the male attraction. They, too, are easier to live with and less likely to develop behavior problems.

TEACHING "PLACE"

Here's an important exercise to begin teaching this week that will give you distance control whenever circumstances dictate the need for it, at home or wherever you go. It's teaching your puppy to go to his "place" and stay there until you release him. His place can be his own

"Go to your place" should be a familiar exercise. It should not be used for disciplinary purposes.

bed, a basket, an old towel, a cushion or whatever you decide to call the control area. It should never be just a particular spot on the floor. It should be an item that can be moved around and taken with you whenever you travel. By having a familiar item that he recognizes as his "place," he will feel secure and comfortable when told, "Go to your place."

First, choose the item that will become his place. I don't recommend using a piece of carpet, because carpeting is stiff and cannot be folded up and carried to various places with ease. A soft blanket or cushion, however, can be tucked under your arm whenever you and your puppy go visiting someone.

Have the puppy on collar and lead, and sit down at a table with the cushion on the floor next to you. Put the puppy on the cushion and tell him to lie down and stay. Fold the lead over your lap so you can grab it quickly when the pup decides to get up and walk away. At first, have the puppy stay in his place for five minutes. Increase the time by five minutes each day until he's staying for 20 or 30 minutes. The goal is for the puppy to stay on his cushion while you eat your dinner. He's nearby, but not interfering with the family members who are eating.

Once the puppy realizes that he must stay in his place until you release him, move the cushion or bed away from you in 2-foot increments. Choose a spot across the room where you'll want him eventually to stay during mealtime. The place should be in the same room with you—far enough away from you that the pup will not interfere with you or the other place, but in a place where he can see you at all times. That way, he'll be content to lie down and rest while you do whatever you need to do without him.

Always end his staying in his place with lots of praise and a food treat. You can even save a small piece of food from your own plate and, when you release your dog, carry the cushion into the kitchen, where you can reward your dog with that special treat. The dog quickly learns that staying on his cushion will produce a wonderful treat when his "place" time ends.

"SIT" WHILE GREETING PEOPLE

Your puppy needs to learn to sit politely beside you whenever he meets other people. You can supply the other person with a biscuit to use as a treat once you get

the dog to sit and wait instead of trying to jump all over the other person. As soon as the other person gives the puppy his treat, you join in with lots of verbal praise. It's important that he knows that you approve of his good manners, too.

TEACH A NEW TRICK

Teach your puppy to hold a biscuit on his nose and wait until you say, "Okay," before he flips it into the air and catches it as it comes down. This will really impress your friends and make your puppy a real star in the neighborhood.

Have the puppy sit facing you. Use a dry dog biscuit rather than a slice of hotdog or cheese. Place your left hand under the dog's chin and lightly grasp his muzzle without squeezing it. With your right hand, place the biscuit on top of the puppy's nose as you keep his muzzle level so the biscuit doesn't slide off. Tell him to "wait" repeatedly as you gently hold his

muzzle with the biscuit on top of it. Count to five and say, "Okay!" excitedly. As you release his muzzle from your left hand, pick up the biscuit with your right hand and raise it a few inches above his head. Now drop the biscuit and as it falls, he'll try to grab it in midair. He'll probably miss several times, but soon he'll begin catching the biscuit before it lands on the floor. Once he does that, he'll begin to anticipate that you're going to raise the biscuit above his head when you say, "Okay!" Once he does that, he'll raise his muzzle upward, thereby flipping the biscuit into the air as you give the go-ahead.

Next, you can teach the puppy to hold the biscuit on his nose for 10 to 15 seconds before you give the okay signal and he flips the biscuit into the air. Some puppies learn this trick in a matter of days. Others take longer. However, all puppies can learn to do it, so be patient and encourage the pup to keep trying.

THINGS TO DO

WEEK 6

- Practice all previous exercises.
- Begin weaning off food with all familiar exercises.
- Talk to your veterinarian about neutering or spaying.
- Teach "Go to your place."
- Teach sit while greeting people.
- Teach a new trick.

Puppy Training
The Seventh Week

TEACH "LEAVE IT"

Throughout the years of teaching dog owners how to train their dogs, people have told me that the two most valuable lessons their puppies learned were the "pass the puppy" game and the "Leave it" exercise. Both exercises give the owner control, whether the puppy is on- or off-lead. In the case of "Leave it," the puppy not only learns to avoid something that could have dangerous consequences but also learns to refocus on you when his attention is drawn elsewhere. This, in itself, is a valuable lesson for the little fellow and allows you to relax when you're out with your puppy.

To the puppy, "Leave it" means to stop doing whatever he's doing immediately. For example, stop barking, stop chasing the cat, stop racing around the house with a sofa cushion in your mouth, stop jumping up on the coffee table to steal a biscuit. It means all of those things and a million more: "Whatever it is you're doing, I want you to stop when I tell you to 'Leave it.'"

To begin teaching "Leave it," have the puppy on collar and lead beside you. Hold the lead short in your left hand and, with your right hand, throw a piece of food onto the floor about three feet in front of the dog. As the dog sees the treat and starts to pull toward it, use a stern voice and say, "No. Leave it!" Say it loud, say it firmly. The secret to success with this exercise is in the way you say "Leave it." If you say it in a calm, whiny way, the dog will not understand the urgency and importance of the command. You must use a loud, stern voice in a tone that says, "Don't you dare touch that food!" Keep repeating the command "Leave it!" and wait until the puppy gives up trying to get the food. You'll know this when there's a slack lead between you. The puppy may even sit down beside you as if to say, "I give up." Allow the puppy to wait 30 seconds or so with that slack lead, and then give him a treat from your hand. Pick up the treat you were using on the floor. Do not let your dog eat what was on the floor. "Leave it" should mean just that, not

Teaching your dog to "leave it" establishes boundaries that will keep him out of trouble and could very well save his life!

A recent incident with one of my students is a perfect example of teaching "Leave it" for a dog's safety. A man was walking his golden retriever one evening when they came upon a fried chicken leg in the footpath. When the dog sniffed at it and opened her mouth to grab it, the man shouted, "Leave it!" Later, the man told me that the never lets his dog eat anything she finds outdoors because he has no way of knowing if the food is safe for her to eat.

"Leave it" could very well save your dog's life, were he attempting to pick up something harmful. It gives you control over everything the pup puts into his mouth.

It was that rule that saved the dog's life that night. The dog was startled and immediately turned away from the meat when her owner ordered her to leave it. Upon closer inspection, the man noticed some blue powder on the meat and became suspicious. Using a tissue from his pocket, he retrieved the meat and took it home. He showed it to his neighbor, who was a laboratory technician. The following day, tests showed the blue powder to be arsenic and further investigation revealed the fact that a neighbor hated dogs and was determined to poison all dogs in his neighborhood. The "Leave it" exercise and the owner's quick reaction had saved the dog's life.

"leave it until I say you can have it." Make it clear that food on the ground should not be eaten. Give him a reward from your hand.

Many times, a puppy will give up trying to reach the food but renew his effort after a momentary pause. Be sure the pup understands that he may not have it. Don't be fooled by a temporary pause in his efforts. Since the puppy is in his seventh week of training now, he is beginning to learn ever faster when you introduce new behaviors. Such is the case with "Leave it." After a day or two of using food and a stern verbal command, switch the object from food to something else that might interest the puppy. A set of keys will interest him when he hears it tinkle as it lands on the floor. A dropped spoon, a pen, or anything else that you would not want your dog to put in his mouth is good for teaching this exercise.

Initially you can give the puppy a treat once he backs away and does not touch the item. Next, change the location of the forbidden item by putting it on a low table, a stool, a step or any other place where the puppy could reach it. Taught correctly, the puppy learns to turn away without question from whatever you order him to avoid. Always praise him for responding quickly and correctly to your "Leave it" order.

AND QUIET, TOO!

Although many trainers recommend teaching the dog a "Quiet" command, the author has found that one of the easiest ways to stop a dog from barking at an oncoming person with a dog is to use "Leave it." As soon as the dog stops barking, tell him he's a good dog and make him sit quietly beside you until the other person and his pet pass by. Many small-breed dogs are "barky" and the "Leave it" exercise teaches them to curb their noisy and irritating habit.

INVOLVING FAMILY MEMBERS

Getting other family members involved in the puppy's training is important. The puppy must learn when he's young that all family members are above him in the order of the household hierarchy. Allowing a dog to manipulate humans and try to rule family members is unacceptable. It simply doesn't work. Unfortunately, I've seen too many potentially good dogs that had to be destroyed because their owners failed to teach them manners.

Begin with the oldest family member and teach that person the puppy's commands and behaviors so that he can manage the dog. Encourage the person to practice with the puppy every day for about a week. We want the puppy to feel comfortable obeying the other person's commands as well as yours.

Introduce the next member to the puppy's routine and repeat the process for a week. Once you've taught all family members how to control and work with the puppy, you'll notice how the dog begins to pay attention to all of you even more. Praise and petting are the puppy's "pay" for being obedient, so be sure that each person offers an appropriate amount of praise when the puppy obeys a command.

To instill these lessons in your puppy, it's important that all family members are onboard and reinforce the skills you've taught him.

GROOMING AND HANDLING PRACTICE

Brushing

This is a fun lesson and one that the puppy will learn to love all his life. Every dog needs grooming, some more than others. A short-coated dog needs a soft bristle brush once or twice a week. This will help eliminate falling hair as well as stimulate the skin for healthy hair growth. In addition, brushing your dog on a regular basis can keep you in touch with his overall condition. You can find parasites or bare areas where the hair doesn't seem to be growing. Those spots should be examined by your veterinarian. Tiny abrasions that could turn into major sores can be detected during brushing. Foreign matter such as pine sap or tar on the pads of his feet can be identified for removal.

Dogs with medium or long coats will require more thorough brushing on a regular basis, usually with a wire brush. Some of the longer coated breeds will need professional grooming every six to eight weeks. Breeds such as the poodle, bichon frise, and most of the terrier breeds need regular grooming. Even the sporting dogs such as golden and labrador retrievers and most of the spaniels require an occasional professional grooming to keep them looking their best and feeling good.

Brushing should begin while the dog is still a puppy. All breeds, regardless of coat length, will need regular grooming and must learn to tolerate it while young.

Regardless of the breed of dog or the eventual length of his coat, begin grooming training now. Have the pup lie down on the floor beside you and brush the hair in the direction of its growth. Brush a small portion of the dog and then stop. Tell him he's a good boy and reward him with a biscuit. Do not attempt to brush out the entire puppy the first day. He will tolerate lying beside you and being brushed for just a short period of time. Each time you brush him, make the process last a little longer and reward him with a treat and praise. Before long, he'll lie there quietly while you brush him all over.

Start early and teach your dog to love grooming. It makes life so much more pleasant when he submits to grooming rather than resists it. After all, it's something he must endure all his life, so he might as well enjoy it!

Foot Care

Have the puppy lie down on the floor beside you while you are sitting on the floor. Pick up one of his front feet and examine it. The whole time you're looking at the foot and nails, tell the puppy what a

Your dog's feet have to be examined, and his nails trimmed on a regular basis. Introduce foot examinations to your puppy from an early age, and eventually your pup will enjoy his pedicures.

pretty foot he has and what a good boy he is. Speak calmly and softly so he learns to relax. Examine the pads of his foot as well as the toenails. When you've examined one foot, stop and reward him with a treat and praise.

The next day, examine foot number two and so on each day until you can examine all four feet at one time. It won't take long for the dog to understand that foot care is fun and rewarding. If you wish to learn how to cut your dog's toenails, have your breeder or veterinarian teach you how to do it. Once you accustom your puppy to having his feet examined, teaching him to allow nail trimming will be easy.

Mouth and Teeth Care

The same approach applies to teaching the puppy to have his mouth and teeth examined. Introduce the examination in short steps and always give a treat and praise at the end. It should take only a matter of a few times and the puppy will learn that opening his mouth while you have a look is OK.

If you want to learn how to brush your puppy's teeth, you can have your veterinarian teach you. You can also purchase a toothbrush and proper toothpaste for dogs from your vet. Be aware that there will be times during your puppy's life when professional teeth cleaning will be necessary. If you begin

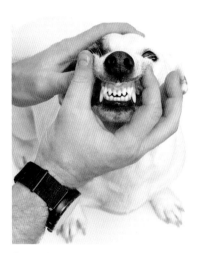
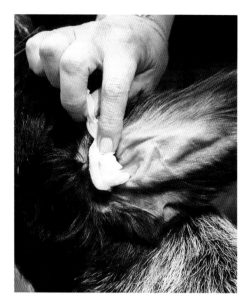

Caring for your puppy's mouth and ears requires only that the puppy becomes accustomed to this type of handling, and that you use a gentle touch.

examining his mouth when he's a puppy, a veterinary exam will be less stressful to him later in life.

Ear Care

Ear care is important, too. Dogs can get ear mites and fungus infections. They can get other kinds of parasites that drive them crazy and cause extreme suffering. In addition, they can get bacterial invasions that cause even more pain and discomfort. Like ourselves, dogs need hygienic care to maintain top physical condition, and keeping them healthy is essential to having happy dogs.

Have your puppy sit or lie down beside you and examine each ear while

FLOP OR UPRIGHT?

Dogs with ears that flop over are prone to all kinds of ear problems if the ears are not kept clean and free of foreign matter. Because closed ear flaps create a warm, dark, moist environment, these dogs are always candidates for trouble. Dogs with upright ears can have ear problems, too, so examining their ears on a regular schedule should be a part of general maintenance procedures.

you speak softly and tell him to stay. Get him accustomed to hearing your gentle comments about how pretty his ears are and how good he is to let you see them. Treats and praise always end the examination and soon he won't mind ear inspections very much at all.

If you notice your puppy's pawing at his ears, rubbing them along the floor or carpet, scratching them or shaking his head constantly, he will need to be seen by your veterinarian. Painful ears aren't fun for anyone, especially your puppy.

INCREASING TIME AND DISTANCE

This week, start adding distance between you and the puppy during your stays. Remember that, eventually, circumstances may require that the dog wait alone for several minutes while you attend to some matter. In order to prepare the puppy for that kind of reliability, begin early in the puppy's life and increase the difficulty in small increments. Begin by giving the puppy a sit-stay with you standing up straight in front of him (no food in your hand) and your open palm facing the dog just like a traffic officer would do when he stops traffic. Stand one yard away from your puppy and return to him after 30 seconds.

Once you've returned to the dog, praise him generously and then produce a biscuit as a special treat. Do not give the

The stay command is given both verbally and with a proper hand signal. Issue the command before you move from beside the pup to out in front of him, and maintain the position of your hand until you return to his side.

food while you're praising. Remember you've weaned the puppy off food in training and your goal is for the puppy to accept praise only as his reward so food treats must be given in a random pattern.

Increase the time and distance that you leave your puppy over the next few weeks. By the end of the first week, you should be able to leave the puppy in a sit-stay while you walk to the opposite end of the room and stay there for one minute. You may need to remind the puppy several times to "stay." As the puppy becomes accustomed to staying in the sit position while you step away from him, begin the same process with the down-stay. As far as the stand-stay is concerned, I don't teach a long stand-stay to the puppy because most of the time in real life when the dog will be required to stand, someone will be with him such as a groomer or veterinarian.

If the puppy breaks either stay, return to him and say, "No. Stay," as you replace him in the required position. If you go back to stand beside him, he'll think the exercise is over and he'll prepare to get up and celebrate. Just return to face him, correct his mistake and go back to where you were originally standing. If the puppy insists that he cannot stay as long as your training schedule calls for, back up to a point in training where he will stay without correction. Never hesitate to back up to an easier step of the exercise because you want the puppy to succeed, not fail.

THINGS TO DO

WEEK

7

- Practice all previous exercises.
- Teach "Leave it."
- Involve family members in the puppy's training.
- Begin grooming practice with brushing, foot care, mouth and teeth care, ear care.
- Increase time and distance in sit- and down-stay exercises.

Puppy Training
The Eighth Week

No doubt you've begun to notice some significant changes in your puppy over these past few weeks. Providing you've done your own homework and taught him his lessons faithfully, plus practiced regularly every day, your puppy is now a responsive, thinking individual. He's learned to learn and to focus on you when you're communicating with him, and he's even begun to use his own behavior to tell you what's going on in his mind. It never fails to excite me when I see a puppy tell me, by his behavior, that he's thinking and making decisions for himself. He may even show that he can solve problems and do things I never dreamed he could do. In short, I'm very proud of this little fellow and you should be just as proud of yours about now.

RETRIEVING

Your puppy's progress gives cause for a new behavior and an exciting new period in his life. It's called retrieving, and the simple act of running after and catching a ball and bringing it back to you can grow

into all manner of sophisticated behaviors. Yet it all begins with a simple principle: the chase instinct.

Since dogs have always been predators, they must run down their prey in order to eat. This chasing instinct is very strong in all breeds, stronger in some. Whatever level of prey drive your puppy possesses, you'll use that chase instinct to teach retrieving. Using force to teach the retrieve is inhumane and frequently backfires to a point of having the dog learn to retrieve but refuse to do it because he dislikes it so much.

Begin by choosing the puppy's favorite toy. Put the puppy on a 10- to 20-foot line so you have control at all times. If you don't, the pup may retrieve the object and then proceed to play cat and mouse with you for hours! After all, he's learned that teasing the boss is so much fun! With the puppy on your left side and the toy in your right hand, hold the line in your left hand. Show the toy to the puppy and wiggle it excitedly as you say "See this? Go get it!"

Teaching your dog to retrieve items is a great way to bond and train while playing.

As soon as the puppy shows interest in the toy, toss it out in front of you about 5 or 6 feet. Let the puppy run after it and grab it. Now use your long line to gently guide the puppy into you as you say, "Bring it here, good boy. Bring it back." As soon as the puppy gets within an arm's length of you, take the toy from him and praise generously. Do not allow the puppy to drop the toy at your feet. Take it quickly before he drops it so he becomes accustomed to having you take it from him.

As you take the toy, say "Out." Eventually the dog will bring back an item and learn to hold it until he hears your command to give it up. Having the dog drop the object means that

The golden retriever requires practically no training to retrieve, although other breeds will require more encouragement to develop this skill.

you'll have to bend down and pick it up before you can throw it again. That, in turn, means the dog is training you! The dog must deliver his retrieved article to your hand.

Never play this retrieve game for too long at any one time. Always quit while the puppy wants you to throw it just one more time. That way, he'll be eager to play it again the next day. From time to time, introduce different articles for retrieving so the puppy gets used to fetching a variety of items. Always be sure that the item is something the dog is capable of handling without becoming discouraged because the object is too heavy or unwieldy.

It may be tempting to play the retrieve game with the puppy off his long line, but don't do it until you're sure he'll come directly back to you. Some puppies like to grab the article and race around the yard to tease the owner. Don't permit this!

If you have bigger plans for your dog when he becomes an adult, and you want him to carry items to help you, make sure that he learns as a beginner that retrieving is great fun but it does have rules. One of those rules is to return the item directly and promptly to you.

In the future, you may become interested in obedience competition, and that will include retrieving exercises. You may also want to train your dog as a helper dog around your home or yard.

You may want him to help carry packages when you go places. All of these behaviors will prove easy to teach if you introduce retrieving as a game to your dog when he is a puppy.

ALTERING UNDESIRABLE BEHAVIORS

When you want to change behaviors you don't like, it's useful to remember that recognizing good behavior and ignoring unwanted behavior is usually the best approach to take. It's a humane way of saying to your puppy, "I don't like what you're doing and I'm going to recognize and reward you when you stop." Remember Thorndike's theory about behavior that results in a pleasant event tending to be repeated?

Let's say, for example, that your puppy is barking unnecessarily while you're sitting and reading. What he's really saying is, "Give me some attention. You're ignoring me and I don't like it." Your behavioral response should say, "I'll be happy to give you my attention, but first you must earn it and barking is not a way to get it." Put your book down and have the puppy do something to earn some attention. Have him do a sit or a down or a sit-stay.

After a short period, release him from the command and give him lots of attention with praise. No food! A few repetitions of that routine will have him

Some puppies are natural retrievers (and even have "retriever" in their names). This labrador retriever puppy is learning about bumpers on the beach.

thinking twice before he demands your attention again. Encouraging him to entertain himself will also help when you tell him to go get his toy and you praise him when he finds it. If you try to correct him for barking for your attention, you'll likely get more barking. That irritation will cause you to give him negative attention that will, in his mind, be better than no attention at all. It's sort of like naughty children who do bad things so people will notice them. Instead of getting recognized for good behavior, they are noticed for their bad behavior.

Your puppy should realize early in life that he must earn the things he wants

Go back to puppy's first lesson and review all the behaviors you've taught him over the past eight weeks. There's a saying about behaviors: "If you don't use it, you'll lose it." Don't let that happen to your dog!

and that nothing in life comes for free. If he believes that you owe him attention, then you have a spoiled dog just as some people have spoiled children who spend their lives demanding from everyone. Having a dog that respects you and his other family members will be a rewarding and wonderful experience for all.

YOUR PUPPY'S MEMORY

There are many things about the canine brain that are similar to the human brain. Memory and how it functions is one of them. Like humans, dogs have short-term memories and long-term memories. When a dog learns something new, he retains the behavior in his short-term memory for only a few hours up to a few days, depending on the individual. However, once he's performed that behavior for approximately 42 days, the behavior switches over to reside in his long-term memory forever.

The best analogy I can give you is the behavior of bike riding in humans. Children learn to ride bikes and do so for many years. Then comes the time when they enter the teen years and cars are on their minds while the bikes get put away. Most teenagers eventually grow up and marry and have children of their own. One day, they purchase bicycles for their own children and, seeing the bike sitting in the yard, they wonder if they can still ride. They get on the bike and immediately pedal away as if they'd ridden a bike just yesterday. Why was it so easy for them to resume riding after all those years?

The answer lies in the long-term memory. Because they had ridden bikes for so long as children, the skill was forever stored in their long-term memories. All it took to recall the memory of how to ride was to get on a bike and ride.

That's what happens with your dog. Teach him something and practice it for about six weeks, and it will be his forever. Like humans, he will only have to hear the command and review the behavior momentarily to regain full performance of it again. That's why people who train their dogs for only two weeks wonder why the dog does not obey commands a year later. The dog didn't have a chance to transfer the knowledge of that behavior into his long-term memory, so it was lost. The older dog who has been doing something for years will never forget. It's stored forever in his long-term memory.

When teaching your puppy to perform whichever behaviors you want him to learn, keep this memory function in mind for the best results over the years. One day it will surprise you when you see your dog do something that you didn't think he'd recall.

ONE MORE TRICK: THE HIGH FIVE

Here's one of the examples of creating a new behavior based on an earlier lesson. Remember during week #4 when we taught the puppy to give you his paw? Not only did it serve as a trick but it also helped introduce nail trimming.

This week, we'll take the simple "Give me your paw" trick and build it into a "High five" trick. This behavior includes the dog's learning to offer you either paw, depending on which hand you offer to him, plus he must learn to put his foot out straight in front of himself instead of placing his paw in your hand.

Begin with a treat in your left hand. Extend your right hand toward the dog's foot but, instead of placing your hand with the palm up, turn your hand so the fingers point up toward the ceiling. As he attempts to place his left paw in your right hand, turn your hand so your palm touches his footpads. Even a slight touch is enough to reward him at first. Progress slowly so he begins to get the idea that when you say "High five," he must extend his left paw to touch the palm of your right hand. A treat always follows, with lots of praise.

Now reverse the process. Hold the treat in your right hand. Extend your left hand toward his right paw and say "High five." Very soon, he'll watch to see which hand you put up in order for him to know which paw to offer for the high five.

Keep in mind two things before beginning this trick: Always have the dog sitting and always have him facing you so that he can easily extend the appropriate paw to connect with your outstretched palm.

THINGS TO DO

WEEK 8

- Teach retrieving.
- Begin altering unwanted behaviors.
- Teach high-five trick.

INDEX

SOME FINAL THOUGHTS

If you and your puppy have worked your way through to this point in the book, I know you two have developed a relationship of trust and understanding that you probably never dreamed possible. In short, you're a team!

As the saying goes, "This is the first day of the rest of your lives together." Congratulations! I wish you both the very best of everything. You deserve it!

PHOTO CREDITS

Photography by Beverly Walter, Isabelle Français and Carol Ann Johnson.

Page 1: New Africa; **Page 7:** Dorottya Mathe; **Page 8:** Anna Hoychuk; **Page 9:** Joca de Jong, KatMoys; **Page 10:**Christian Mueller; **Page 11:** belefront; **Page 12:** BarboraChr; **Page 13:** gillmar; **Page 15:** Artsiom P; **Page 16:** J.A. Dunbar; **Page 17:** otsphoto; **Page 18:** Bulltus_casso; **Page 21:** pets and foods; **Page 22:** Christine Bird; **Page 23:** koshkin stock; **Page 24:** thka; **Page 26:** Michael Kraus, Viorel Sima; **Page 27:** karen roach; **Page 28:** Weerameth Weerachotewong; **Page 29:** bmf-foto.de; **Page 30:** Zhitkov Boris; **Page 31:** New Africa; **Page 32:** Zachary Hoover; **Page 35:** ANURAK PONGPATIMET; **Page 37:** BG-FOTO; **Page 38:** Ilya Soldatkin; **Page 39:** ABO Photography; **Page 40:**Christian Mueller; **Page 42:** Csanad Kiss; **Page 43:** Lopolo; **Page 45:** Wasitt Hemwarapornchai; **Page 46:** Welshea; **Page 47:** Alena Ivochkina; **Page 48:** Rita_Kochmarjova; **Page 49:** etreeg; **Page 50:** MirasWonderland; **Page 53:** dogboxstudio; **Page 55:** Annorak Nk, Chekyravaa; **Page 56:** Aleksey Boyko, ABO Photography, Olga Kri; **Page 58:** sophiecat, chrisukphoto; **Page 59:** Stone36; **Page 60:** Serhii Bobyk, Reddogs, Aleksey Boyko; **Page 61:** 9gifts, otsphoto, ValeriyPH; **Page 62:** Nina Buday; **Page 63:** Zanna Pesnina; **Page 66:** Switlana Sonyashna; **Page 68:** Anna Hoychuk; **Page 69:** Anna Hoychuk, MirasWonderland; **Page 71:** TeamDAF; **Page 74:** thka, Three Dogs photography; **Page 75:** thka; **Page 76:**Ovchinnikova; **Page 77:** virgmos; **Page 78:** Zamrznuti tonovi; **Page 79:** Artsiom P; **Page 80:** Kseniya Ivanova; **Page 81:**SasaStock; **Page 83:** cynoclub; **Page 86:** GaudiLab; **Page 87:** Andrea Izzotti; **Page 88:** ANURAK PONGPATIMET; **Page 89:** Yekatseryna Netuk, Masarik; **Page 91:** Javier Brosch; **Page 94:** Javier Brosch, thka; **Page 95:**Aarontphotography; **Page 97:** leeactor; **Page 101:** New Africa, ARTSILENSE; **Page 103:** Piotr Piatrouski; **Page 105:**Christine Bird; **Page 106:** Angela Holmyard; **Page 107:** Gladskikh Tatiana; **Page 108:** Lopolo; **Page 109:** Patryk Kosmider; **Page 111:** Ermolaev Alexander; **Page 112:** NotarYES; **Page 113:** Media Home; **Page 114:** My Good Images; **Page 115:** Firuza39; **Page 116:** amedeoemaja; **Page 117:** Ekaterina43; **Page 119:** Ekaterina Kamenetsky; **Page 121:**Master1305; **Page 125:** Yellow Cat.